Success by
Another Measure

4790-PAWL

Success by Another Measure

RECOGNIZING AND ENHANCING YOUR CHARACTER

Robert E. Pawlicki, Ph.D.

790-PAWL

To order additional copies of this book, contact:
Xlibris Corporation
1-888-7-XLIBRIS
www.Xlibris.com
Orders@Xlibris.com

Contents

TO MY GRANDFATHER, INNOCENZO ROSSITTO,
WHO TAUGHT ME THE
IMPORTANCE OF EDUCATION

TO MY MOTHER AND FATHER,
MARIE AND TONY PAWLICKI,
WHOSE LOVE LAID THE
FOUNDATION FOR GROWTH

Author's Note

ALL references to patients seen in therapy cited in this book
have been modified to protect their privacy and anonymity.
Therefore, any similarity between the names and stories of
individuals described in this book and individuals known to
the reader is purely coincidental.

**The greatest good you can do for
another is not just to share your riches,
but to reveal to him his own.**

Benjamin Disreali

Preface

Success by Another Measure is based on the assumption that, underneath an avalanche of media images of a people seeking material wealth, there is another America. This America is made up of people who are good, caring, and behaving in a fashion that should be recognized and honored. It is based on the assumption that clarifying personal qualities is valuable. Once our beliefs and attributes are labeled, each person gains meaning and direction in his life.

To fully understand our own character takes work. *Success by Another Measure* provides a structure for that work. Chapters one through eight emphasize the importance of character, provide a definition and give examples of wonderful expressions of character. Character is learned and can be cultivated. It is acquired through examples, lessons, models and beliefs passed on from those around us. Overtly and covertly we are shaped to a set of values that is uniquely our own. But, since this composite of values is learned and not inherited like eye color, it can be magnified, solidified, cultivated, reinforced or ignored.

The heart of any motivational book is its ability to inspire change. And the heart of *Success by Another Measure* is its ability to stimulate change through thought and action. The thought is initially in the form of engaging in the exercises provided. These exercises increase awareness of personal make-up. Subsequent action takes the form of carrying over new perceptions to daily life and allowing new found awareness to solidify or shape individual character. One begins by introspection, turning attention to a focus on character, and reflecting on critical questions. It is through the contemplation of the book's examples, response to important questions and exercises, that the discovery of underlying character will occur.

In the second section of *Success by Another Measure*, the focus turns to self-esteem and personal considerations. Often self-esteem has appeared in the self-improvement literature as the source of mental health. While undoubtedly critical, self-esteem is more related to personality than to character — more related to the outer shell than the inner core. Nevertheless, the outer shell is important and does need attention. Chapter 9 focuses on practical means to bolster and maintain good self-esteem.

The last chapter of the book briefly details some the personal challenges I have faced. I discuss the fallibility of simple answers to complex problems and encourage the reader to be patient with himself. I ask the reader to return during life's challenges to his or her basic character, to that set of values uncovered in these pages.

Section One

RECOGNIZING YOUR CHARACTER

Chapter 1

WHAT IS CHARACTER

PSYCHOLOGISTS aren't supposed to cry after the patient leaves the office. After all, we hear hundreds of stories that are tragic, sad and depressing. We're supposed to build up an emotional veneer that protects both our inner self and our ability to treat great numbers of patients.

Martha penetrated that veneer. I first saw her about fourteen years ago, referred by her family physician for the management of a diabetic neuropathy pain in her lower right leg. However, this constant burning pain did not turn out to be the subject of our discussion. It was Martha's personal story that was even more devastating than her painful leg. Martha had lost five members of her family in the proceeding month. On June 3rd, her mother died of cancer. On the 6th, her husband died of a massive heart attack. On the 13th, she witnessed the murder of her son in front of her eyes. One week later, her father died in her arms, and on the 28th, her sister died in an automobile accident. Martha slowly described each one of these events in significant detail. When she left my office, I felt both depleted and terribly sad. So much so that I went into the next room and cried, hard. Martha was nice, kind and not someone who deserved such tragedy.

My next patient was not so kind. As a matter of fact, she was quite immature, even whiny and certainly not very responsible. Nevertheless, she sat in front of me terribly depressed. It was her birthday and no one had sent her a birthday card. Now this young woman had no idea of the experience of the preceding patient, but I did and I had to hold myself back from grabbing her by the collar and shaking her. "Don't you have any idea how insignificant not receiving a birthday card is in the great picture of your life?" I wanted to say.

I am a psychologist trained in pain management techniques and this woman had come to be treated for pain and depression. The pain was from a crushing injury to her little finger suffered in a work-related accident. The dimension of both her physical and emotional injuries seemed trivial in comparison to Martha's. But it made no difference. This young woman was suffering as much, if not more, than the patient whose experiences had touched me so deeply. This woman, overwrought and desperately sad, was teaching me a lesson that has been supported hundreds of times since. The degree of our sadness and happiness is *within* our being. It is not a result of the events that happen to us. It is how we perceive and manage these events that is the most critical factor and, fortunately, the one that we can control. I have since had to remind myself of that lesson often, for it is an easy one to forget. It is difficult to remember in considering the feelings of others and perhaps even more difficult to remember in ourselves.

In ensuing years I have come to understand a second lesson from my two patients. It is simply that some people bring to the table of life a set of values, principles and beliefs—character—that steel them against life's difficulties. This strength does not stem from better problem solving skills, better genes, or greater luck. While each of these advantages may help, it is the underlying core of each individual, their character, that will determine their reaction to the challenges of life.

Martha had character. When I saw her, she was in an early and appropriate stage of grieving. But when she detailed her other life experiences, I saw fortitude, courage, integrity, and perseverance. She described a family closeness to which she gave in abundance and from which she took sustenance. Whether it was fair or not, I could easily empathize with her because of who she was—a women of character. Faced with a life experience few of us could imagine, her character would pull her through.

Author Stephen Covey points out that material written for self-improvement books before the turn of the century was based largely on the development of character instead of the more recent emphasis upon personality. In an expression of the earlier time, character had to do with the "fundamentals of the person"—those things which answered the question of personal identity.

While there may not be a plethora of 20th century books extolling the value of character, there is no shortage of extraordinary examples of people of character. In World War II, a war that lasted almost four years for American forces, President Franklin Delinor Roosevelt was greatly troubled by the loss of American life. But it was often said that his sense of purpose never wavered. During the dark days when American solders were pushed back at the Battle of the Bulge with horrible losses, many Americans despaired. Not so Roosevelt. His optimism, beliefs and sense of purpose were unflagging and historians say that this sense of steadfastness and determination of purpose gave great strength to the American people. Roosevelt's friend and Secretary of State,

General George Marshall was to declare, "In great stress, Roosevelt was a strong man."[1]

Nelson Mandela spent twenty-seven years of his life in prison—twenty-seven years during the prime of his life. In his autobiography he states that he did not touch his wife for twenty-one years. What could possibly sustain a man through this extraordinary period of hardship? Undoubtedly, it was his sense of purpose.

These examples shout out as illustrations of "walking your talk." But what does that mean? One has to know what his talk is—not just an amorphous notion of life's purpose, but a definition of personal purpose. Not a response in the negative—a response of what one is against—but a clear affirming statement of one's personal direction—answers to the question "who are you?" and "what do you stand for?"

Why should an individual of strong moral fiber handle stress any differently from a person of lesser strength? Strength of character denotes principle, purpose, and perspective. Character provides guidance during periods of stress. Consider Harry Truman, for example. Whatever their opinion of his politics, people who knew him greatly admired his character. Perhaps nowhere was the character of the man better expressed than in a prayer he is reported to have memorized and recited throughout much of his life:

> *"Oh, Almighty and Everlasting God, Creator of Heaven, Earth and the Universe:*
> *Help me to be, to think, to act what is right, because it is right; make me truthful, honest and honorable in all things; make me intellectually honest for the sake of right and honor and without thought of reward to me. Give me the ability to be charitable, forgiving and patient with my fellowmen—help me to understand their motives and their shortcomings—even as Thou understandest mine!*

Amen, Amen, Amen."[2]

These values and qualities of character differ from personality in their depth. Personality is readily visible, the exterior, the apparent. It can change as a function of the environment and the role one plays. Not so character. Character is a constant. Persons imbued with honesty, integrity, fidelity, fairness, and honor don't exhibit these characteristics at home but not at work; with friends but not with strangers; with people of similar background, but not so with those who differ.

Character is an inner quality that speaks of a personal strength, a set of beliefs and internal dialog. In discussing the courageous acts of great American statesmen in withstanding the barbs, criticisms and downright aggression of their colleagues and constituents, John F. Kennedy, in his Pulitzer Prize winning book *Profiles in Courage*, writes:

> *"It was not because they 'loved the public better than themselves.' On the contrary it was precisely because they did love themselves—because each one's need to maintain his own respect for himself was more important to him than his popularity with others—because his desire to win or maintain a reputation for integrity and courage was stronger than his desire to maintain his office—because his conscious, his personal standards of ethics, his integrity or morality, call it what you will—was stronger than the pressures of public disapproval—because his faith that his course was the best one, and would ultimately be vindicated, outweighed his fear of public reprisal."*[3]

Where does character come from? In another age it was overtly taught, thought to be the inner core of what was to be valued in a man or a woman. Taught by lessons at home and school. Taught by stories illustrating moral principles. Taught by example. Harry Truman was brought up in one such age. In the following excerpt biographer David McCullough details how Truman (born in 1884) was schooled:

> *"Certain precepts and bywords were articles of faith in such a place (Independence, Missouri), in such times, and nearly everybody growing up there was imbued with them, in principle at least. Honesty was the best policy. It saved time and worry, because if you always told the truth you never had to keep track of what you said. Make yourself useful. Anything worthwhile required effort. If at first you don't succeed, try again. 'Never, never give up,' Harry's father would say. Children were a reflection of their parents. 'Now Harry, you be good,' his mother would tell him time after time after he went out the door."[4]*

Speaking of his schoolteachers Truman would write,

> *"They gave us our high ideals, and they hardly ever received more than forty dollars a month."* According to Truman, they taught the old rooted values—loyalty, love of home, unquestioning patriotism—no less than Latin, history, or Shakespeare.[5]

Character is learned not only during the critical window of youth. Certainly having character taught early and often can offer great advantages. But human beings are adaptable. We can learn at any age.

Some will argue that Mahatma Gandhi represents the finest of moral leadership in the twentieth century. But he too was still honing his own character as an adult. Imprisoned in a cell in South Africa, Gandhi read works of great literature, cultivating his own philosophy. Writing to his seventeen-year-old son, he states:

*"All confirm the view that education does not mean
knowledge of letters but it means character building."*

If Gandhi is to be believed, character can be developed. Like all things of value, it is not easily acquired, but attainable it is. For most of us it is not a matter of starting from zero. Since character is basic we are more likely to discover it within ourselves and build it than to create it anew. By asking the appropriate questions and directing our focus in the proper direction we may be surprised to find the substance of character within us already.

It would be rare to find a reader who would admit to a lack of character, but it is very common to find those who struggle with statements of personal identity and character. It is my belief that the clarification of our personal identity, an increased awareness of our character, and a refinement of the direction we seek to travel will do more to enhance our abilities to manage the difficulties of our lives than any other pursuit. I believe that an increased awareness of the qualities that make up our character allows for a sensitivity to personal actions that further enhances values and principles. And I believe that clarification of identity and character gives us greater meaning in life.

This book is written for those on the quest of cultivating their character. Two steps are necessary in this effort. The first is to search out your own character, identifying with greater clarity who you are. Secondly, I believe each of us benefits by developing a plan and a commitment for further growth of our character. These two steps are intertwined and interlocking. We will focus on each of the two steps on our journey.

The United States is an extraordinary country. Its people are dynamic and basically good. Born two hundred years ago in a document that promised dignity and worthiness to every citizen, it has surpassed every other nation in its opportunity for well-being. In the twentieth century it has emerged as the most powerful nation in the world and is the foremost leader in economic growth, entertainment, sports, electronics, food production and many, many other areas.

During this last century it has stood as the antithesis of totalitarianism, dictatorship and communism. In these areas the enemy has been clear and the objective plain. As we move into the twenty-first century a new enemy has emerged, however, one much less obvious and much more insidious. The enemy is the gradual deterioration of our individual and national character.

In the new millennium we must acknowledge that our individual character is being eroded by another force—the attraction of materialism. Our quest for the "better life" in the form of material gain has too often distracted us from the qualities of character that brought the U.S. to the world's forefront: courage, fairness, honesty, integrity, openness, hard work, and so on.

Three decades ago Martin Luther King stood before a nation and spoke these words:

> *"So I say to you, my friends, that even though we must face the difficulties of today and tomorrow, I still have a dream. It is a dream deeply rooted in the American dream that one day this nation will rise up and live out the true meaning of its creed—we hold these truths to be self-evident, that all men are created equal."*

We too must have a dream—a dream that is not fulfilled by

richness of goods but by richness of character—a dream in which we believe in our individual worthiness and dignity. A dream that nourishes acts which make us proud.

Dreams can be achieved with hard work and self-discipline. We, as a nation, are fortunate, for we have a history of dreams, self-discipline and hard work. Periodically, however, we lose our way. And the task at hand may be, in many ways, much more difficult than past problems in which the issues were clear and external. It is always easier to mobilize energy and force against threats from the outside. The threat of shallowness of character within our being, however, is more challenging and, indeed, more formidable. Nevertheless, our personal, family, community, and nation's well-being is dependent upon our attention to those qualities which form the basis of who we are and what we stand for.

The good of the individual and the good of the community are inextricably tied. We, as a country, are among the most individualistic of nations. We take pride in our individualism and cite the independence of our heroes, the pioneer, the cowboy and the scientist working steadfastly in the laboratory. Daniel Boone, Buffalo Bill and Thomas Edison speak to the American spirit. Our laws are geared to protect individual rights and often encourage the freedom of the one to the detriment of the whole. Contrasted with countries such as Japan, where community mores are paramount, Americans can sometimes appear reckless and undisciplined. While we come together for the common good during periods of crisis such as war, we struggle during other times focused on individual gains to the impairment of our national welfare. The idea of coming together, the idea of community is foreign to a large portion of our population except in times of trouble. My belief is that such a time exists now. I believe we have fallen into a pattern of individualism, fed by materialism, that distracts us from another of American's basic values—the need to do the right thing, to be good for its own sake.

In this book I write of personal character. I salute character as the fundamental building block of personal well-being, and real success—success defined to include goodness. I believe that personal character is the best starting point for the building of foundations for all other institutions critical to our country's well being—family (defined to include multiple variations), friendship, local and national community. When individuals discover and enhance their own character, when each of us learns to take care of our own needs in a healthy fashion, we create humans who are capable of greater generosity, tolerance and kindness. We move away from insecurities and fears that nourish selfishness, deceit and intolerance.

Former President Clinton spoke in a 1997 speech of the intertwining of individual freedom and group responsibility:

> *"Take a penny from your pocket. On one side, next to Lincoln's portrait, is a single word: 'Liberty.' On the other side is our national motto. It says 'E Pluribus Unum—Out of Many, One.' It does not say 'Every Man for Himself.' That humble penny is an explicit declaration—one you can carry around in your pocket—that America is about both individual liberty and community obligation. These two commitments— to protect personal freedom and seek common ground— are the coin of the realm, the measure of our worth."*

We need both attention to ourselves and attention to the needs of the community. But we are most likely to reach the loftiest mountain and to achieve our greatest communal goals when we begin from a position of personal strength—from a position of character. It is for this reason that I ask you to begin your journey with me in this book with the following commitment:

I commit myself to take care of myself for the sake of myself, my family, my friends, my community and my country.

Chapter 2

IDENTIFYING YOUR CHARACTER

FOR twenty years I have listened to the stories of people in chronic pain—every type of pain one can imagine. Pain with fancy names like Reflex Sympathetic Dystrophy, Diabetic Neuropathy, Fibromyalgia, Myofascia Pain Syndrome, and on and on. Pain in every part of the body from the head to the toes, in the elbows, neck, face, knees, genitals, buttocks and, of course, the back. Pain with a clear diagnosis and pain of unknown origin or source.

I have listened to untold stories of suffering. Suffering in the form of depression, anxiety, anger, uncertainty and loneliness. Suffering that appeared needless, unfair, unjust and terribly sad. I have observed the strong, courageous, de-termined, and resourceful as well as the weak, timid, hesi-tant and helpless. I have watched literally thousands of good human beings of all races and classes struggle with one of life's greatest challenges—unrelenting pain.

Pain and suffering are not the same. Pain, regardless of its source, can be uncomfortable, troublesome, excruciating. Except for its ability to signal some underlying damage, pain has few redeeming qualities. When pain is chronic, even its one advantage—that it is a signal of underlying damage—is lost.

In the world of rehabilitation and more specifically, chronic pain, there is an axiom that is taught: "Pain is inevitable, suffering is optional." This statement conveys the notion that there are pains (psychological and physical) that must be endured. It is our response to pain that is within our control. It is our response, our suffering, that is within our ability to manipulate. In one sense, all management of chronic pain is not really pain management. It is actually suffering management.

In our modern society we have come to use another term for the daily experience of pain—stress. While not connoting the same level of intensity, stress carries with it many of the characteristics of pain. Listen to descriptions of stress and see how they remind you of pain: "anxiety, burden, pressure, frustration, anger." These are the terms I hear patients use in describing their experience of pain. Indeed, beyond the physical attributes, the most debilitating and therefore frustrating element of pain is its ability to interfere with activities of life. The most debilitating characteristic of stress is that it leads to inability to control one's life.

Think about the situations we find stressful. Common everyday experiences—traffic, annoying telephone calls, unwanted noise, smoke, interruptions. Think of the more intense stressors—difficulties with finances, relationships, careers, loneliness and uncertainty. Each stressor carries with it the quality of lack of control. The very essence of stress is lack of control and the very essence of its opposite, tranquility, is control. When we feel the most stressed, we feel helpless.

Libraries and bookstores are filled with material citing the harmful effects of stress on modern America and extensive remedies to manage that stress. Indeed the concept of "stress" has become synonymous with any extended problem. Given the rapid pace and the complexity of our society, it is no wonder that we are inundated with information as to how we can reduce stress.

Most of the traditional recommendations, however, have three major shortcomings: they are reactive, crisis-oriented and often situation specific. Take, for example, the advice you may have been given by friends to manage your stress (such as changing jobs or getting a divorce). Such advice is obviously temporary in nature and often causes more difficulties in the long run.

Or one might manage stress by beginning an educational effort or starting a new behavior. Engaging in a new computer class, aerobics training, communication education and the multitude of other healthy educational efforts has much merit. In many circumstances such activity is appropriate. However, such efforts fail to provide significant stress reduction for the more pervasive and intransigent of life's problems. For these (the ongoing relationship, career, financial, and existential issues of life) we often turn to therapy and the self-help literature. Here, too, we find useful information for many of life's crises. In meaningful therapy, for example, serious and basic changes in perception, attitude, and behaviors can, and often do, occur.

The problem with each of the above approaches is that each tends to focus on a crisis issue at hand and to be reactive in nature. It takes little logic to argue that prevention in virtually all problem areas is more valuable than is remedy. "An once of prevention is worth a pound of cure" is so obvious as to sound trite. However, it is exactly this principle which makes the clear identification of character, the most constructive action we can take to manage the difficulties of life.

Uncovering and developing your character does not need to be done during moments of anxiety, depression, loneliness or fear. Nor does it end once a crisis is over. It is not a remedy only for those who are physically or psychologically unhealthy. It is simply a wise investment for each and every one of us, regardless of our current state. It differs from the aforementioned approaches in that it is a lifelong process, not crisis oriented. It is proactive, not reactive. It is general and adaptive to many circumstances, not confined to specific circumstances.

Whatever value traditional stress-reduction approaches merit, a more sensible approach in managing the stresses of our life would include prevention, proactivity, and long-term perspective. These qualities are inherent in the development of character. I am not proposing that character development be perceived strictly as a remedy, a palliative to life's challenges. Such benefit is only one quality of character development. The development of a strong set of moral values, the identification of a personal set of principles offer an inherent satisfaction in itself. Knowing what one stands for provides meaning and that alone is full justification for the pursuit of character.

Uncovering your character is not as simple as it may seem. Most people have difficulty even stating their identity (answering the question "Who are you?") and struggle even more concerning their character. The question of identity typically refers to personality and role, whereas character refers to personal qualities and principles. While identity and character overlap, we are more familiar with questions concerning identity. But even here the questions stimulate more introspection than most people are equipped to handle.

When I ask patients their identity ("Who are you?"), they usually struggle with the answer. After some hesitation, most answer with their occupation or primary role. When I inquire further regarding their character ("Tell me about the real you—the special qualities that make you, you") most are even more dumbfounded. When I follow their often uncertain response with questions such as, "Are you unreliable, dishonest? Can you be trusted?" their reply is much more definite. "Of course not. No, no, I'm honest. I'm very trustworthy. People know I keep my word." It seems that we have knowledge of our character, lying dormant, in need of cultivation. With some effort we can begin to bring these qualities into sight.

Character is difficult to find. It seems less talked about than in the past. Character is deeper, initially less visible than the roles we play in life. For most of us other people's character is revealed only with time and circumstance. But only to the observant. Knowledge of our own character may be even more difficult to discover. For we may not choose to look, and when we do, our vision is often obscured by fears, doubts and subjectivity.

Webster's Third New International Dictionary defines character as "a composite of good moral qualities typically of moral excellence and firmness blended with resolution, self-discipline, high ethics, force and judgment." A composite of good moral qualities? Yes, but which moral qualities? Is there a set list? Benjamin Franklin made a fine list which he measured himself against for the better portion of his life. The Boy and Girl Scouts have their list stated in their creed. No, there is no absolute list but few would quibble with the list most of us would put forth. Moral excellence clearly excludes the "seven deadly sins" and distinctly includes attributes such as: honest, trustworthy, respectful, honorable, kind, fair, sensitive, forgiving, generous, charitable, responsible, good-humored, and so forth. Your list would be different from mine but undoubtedly admirable. What is critical is that we each establish our own unique set of "good moral values"—and that we live by this composite of qualities to define our character.

Knowing and being able to describe your character in detail has considerable merit. The most important advantage is that, quite simply, it gives you direction. Consider a young adolescent girl, brought up in a structured household, who has consistently defined herself as capable, honest and trustworthy. Ponder what such a young woman who has inculcated these labels into her being is likely to be thinking during a moment of challenge so frequently experienced by today's teenagers. Her internal language will be influenced by her knowledge that certain impulses will go against her picture of who she is and what she stands for. This resulting dissonance will guide her action. A similar young woman who may have as much capability, honesty and trustworthiness, but who has not come to label herself as such, may struggle in this same circumstance.

As humans we seek to maintain harmony—harmony with our internal picture of who we are and for what we stand. If that picture is ambiguous we will experience great struggle. If that picture is blank we will experience still greater struggle.

Consider the extraordinary actions forty years ago of Rosa Parks, a quiet seamstress and one of the most respected black women in Montgomery, Alabama. Her refusal to engage in a segregationist law of her time stirred the black community and precipitated a nonviolent bus boycott. When asked why she had refused to move to the rear of the bus, she said: "It was a matter of dignity; I could not have faced myself and my people if I had moved."[6]

Her reflections came from a sense of who she was and what she stood for. Rosa Parks had been schooled to believe in her dignity—that she was as good as any one else.

Character provides guidelines. An understanding of who I am and what I stand for provides instruction as I maneuver through the decisions of my life. Do I backbite my co-worker to advance my position? Do I tell my spouse of my impulsive spending? Do I share that "juicy" secret my close friend just told me? Each action depends upon your internal guideline or lack there of. There is greater likelihood that a person who strongly and overtly believes himself to be fair, honest and trustworthy will answer the above questions differently from another whose awareness of his personal qualities is less.

Strength of character means a commitment to personal qualities. A commitment, in turn, means a willingness to act consistently with the quality during periods of challenge. Am I fair, honest or charitable when it is convenient or can I uphold these qualities when it is difficult? Again a sense that certain qualities have been imbued into my being to the point that I am synonymous with those characteristics will make it likely that I will continue to act in a consistent manner. If those qualities are ones that I can articulate they become all the more solidified. To act inconsistently with what I believe I am causes disharmony and discomfort. To clarify one's understanding of the qualities that are the make-up of one's personal character therefore strengthens that character.

A strong sense of character influences your thoughts, actions and even your feelings. Examine again the courageous action of Mrs. Parks. Acting consistently with her personal beliefs provided her with feelings of worthiness and pride. To be sure, other feelings such as fear and discomfort can enter into difficult situations. But actions consistent with stated values provide a sense of well-being.

In 1956 Martin Luther King described the thinking, emotions and actions of blacks who showed character by their participation in the bus boycott:

> *"In Montgomery we walk in a new way. We hold our heads in a new way. Even the Negro reporters who*

converged on Montgomery have a new attitude. One
tired reporter, asked at a luncheon in Birmingham to
say a few words about Montgomery, stood up, thought
for a moment, and uttered one sentence: 'Montgomery
has made me proud to be a Negro.'"[7]

Perhaps the most valuable aspect of character is that it provides *internal* control—the most priceless protection we have in defense of stress and pain. Character appears in the midst of the greatest tragedies of our times and one of the most dramatic illustrations appeared in the writing of Viktor Frankl.

Frankl was a Jewish psychiatrist imprisoned in Auschwitz for three years, experiencing the unimaginable. With over 8000 deaths in concentration camps every day, with the chance of surviving roughly 1 in 28, with unspeakable bestial horrors occurring daily, Frankl was asked to speak to his fellow prisoners during one of the darkest days. He spoke of the most trivial of comforts, quoted Nietzsche ("That which does not kill me, makes me stronger"), spoke of the future, mentioned the past with all of its joys and finally spoke of "our sacrifice, which has meaning in every case." Here he is, in a hell most of us cannot imagine, and he speaks of hope. It is his recognition that his captors can take away every visible substance, but they do not control and cannot take away his dignity or his sense of meaning in life. He writes:

> *"The purpose of my words was to find a full meaning*
> *in our life, then and there, in that hut and in that*
> *practically hopeless situation. I saw that my efforts*
> *had been successful. When the electric bulb flared up*
> *again, I saw the miserable figures of my friends limp-*
> *ing toward me to thank me with tears in their eyes."*

Frankl was fond of quoting Nietzche's "He who has a why to live can bear with almost any how." When alone in the concentration camp all goals of life were taken away. What remained was the "last of human freedoms—the ability to choose one's attitude in a given set of circumstances."[8]

Taking control of what is available to us takes many forms. Do you know that Helen Keller, blind and deaf, graduated from Radcliffe College in 1904? At a time when the odds of any woman graduating from college were astronomically low, here we have a woman, deaf and blind, who passed her entrance examination in elementary and advanced German, French, Latin, English, Greek and Roman History. Scholars have marveled at her memory and intellect but just as admirable was her sense of optimism. Greatly limited by her deficits, she nevertheless viewed life from the perspective of joy and challenge. The human animal can reach heights difficult to comprehend. Read Helen Keller describing her teacher Annie Sullivan:

"It was my teacher's genius, her quick sympathy, her loving tact which made the first years of my education so beautiful. It was because she seized the right moment to impart knowledge that made it so pleasant and acceptable to me. She realized that a child's mind is like a shallow brook which ripples and dances merrily over the stony course of its education and reflects here a flower, there a bush, yonder a fleecy cloud; and she attempted to guide my mind along its way, knowing that like a brook it should be fed by mountain streams and hidden springs, until it broadened out into a deep river, capable of reflecting in its placid surface, billowy hill, the luminous shadows of trees and the blue heavens, as well as the sweet face of a little flower."[9]

This paragraph was written by a totally deaf and blind woman in her autobiography published when she was 21 years of age. This amazing woman cultivated the gifts available to her in life, admirable intelligence and sensitivity, to a level that shame those of us dealing with much lesser deficits. The Bible says, "A man cried because he had no shoes, until he saw a man who had no feet." Helen Keller did not feel sorry for herself. She controlled what she could and made the most of it.

Mahatma Gandhi is another human being who inspires and his life attests to the capacity of character and spirit. He repeatedly told those around him that he was in control, not the British. His belief, in the face of total British administrative charge of his country, seemed ludicrous. Not so to Gandhi. His notion was not passive resistance but active resistance, meant to provoke the British and to make England and the world aware of the injustice in the British occupation of India. Throughout his life, riddled with personal hardship and over seven years of imprisonment, Gandhi felt a sense of personal control—control of his thoughts and his actions.

On one occasion, brought before a British magistrate on the charge of sedition, Gandhi stated:

> *"I will save the court time, my lord, by stating under oath that to this day I believe noncooperation with evil is a duty and that British rule is evil."*

Asked what was his defense, Gandhi replies:

> *"I have no defense, my lord, I'm guilty as charged and if you truly believe in the system of law you administrate in my country, you must inflict on me the severest penalty possible."* [10]

Once committed to his code, his path was clear. He was in charge.

Managing stress does not mean eliminating the cause. It means adjusting, adapting, learning, and growing in the face of the stressor. It means character. It means more than survival but actually a strengthening. It is the ability to find meaning in the difficulties and suffering of life that provides strength. (Martin Luther King was fond of saying that "Suffering is redemptive.") It can be said that a measure of a person is found in his ability to manage his or her suffering. Not all people do learn and rarely is there one who does not falter from time to time. But the formidable exceptional individuals who do, in fact, gain strength from their trials are well worth noting.

When we examine their lives there is no constant pattern of personality, skill or style that cuts across greatness and character. Rather it is the ability to adjust, adapt, learn and grow. It is the constant of character. It is their commitment to personal principle. Examining the lives of men and women whose lives reflect character makes sense of who they are.

It should be clear that character does not totally protect one from stress. Character provides an inner strength, guidelines, direction and a measure of control. But life is complex and presents each of us with unique challenges, well illustrated in the life of Robert E. Lee.

When the Civil War started, Lee faced an acute moral conflict. President Lincoln had offered him the command of the Northern forces and he could have taken it on principle, feeling very strongly that secession was wrong. But all his loyalties and affections were with the South. According to historians he spent a day and a night pacing his room deciding how to resolve this dilemma. He said to his son that he believed in the Union, but a Union that can only be held together by swords and bayonets "has no charm for me."[11]

Robert E. Lee commanded respect, even reverence from his troops. The great issues of his time were placed squarely on his shoulders and his personal resolution was born of significant struggle. It is of no small meaning that the general who lost the war is perhaps the soldier we remember the most. It is his character that stands so tall.

Harry S. Truman, Mahatma Gandhi, Viktor Frankl, Helen Keller, Robert E. Lee, Rosa Parks and the civil rights activists all evidenced character. For each, it may have taken a different form. Courage, fortitude, integrity, perseverance and optimism are just some of the qualities displayed. But we are not on the world stage. Our lives may be more simple, less dramatic. Our successes and failures are of less magnitude. Nevertheless, our qualities and our behaviors are important. We face challenges that in our inner being, perhaps our soul, feel as difficult, as challenging, as formidable, as any faced by the giants of history. And if we are to meet these challenges successfully and with goodness, we must face them with character.

To put momentous actions on paper is to illustrate a point. But character is not just great actions during tempestuous times. It is the everyday act performed in the quiet of the day. It is, as Dwight L. Moody has stated, "what you are in the dark," or what Lord Macaulay referred to when he wrote: "The measure of a man's real character is what he would do if he knew he would never be found out."

To face life's challenges with character, we must move from the abstract to the practical. We must identify who we are and what we stand for. No small task.

Assessing your current state and setting up a structure for further growth are wise practical steps in the development of character. As in many endeavors, the first step may be hardest and requires some introspection. The exercise I suggest involves examining those things that you value most in your life. To stimulate such thoughts, take a few moments to complete the following exercise:

Examining Important Priorities In Your Life

1. List the three material items you value most in the world.

A.

B.

C.

2. List the 3 beliefs or values that are most dear to you. (for example: your belief in honesty, God, democracy)

A.

B.

C.

3. List the 3 relationships that you value the most.

A.

B.

C.

You now have a total of nine items listed. Take the nine items and prioritize them in terms of importance to you. If you were in a desperate, perhaps dying situation, and had to forsake two items each day for four days, what would be the first to go and what would be the last? Take the time to actually prioritize your list and then imagine eliminating two each day for four days:

9. (First to be dropped from your life)
8.
7.
6.
5.
4.
3.
2.
1. (Last to be dropped from your life)

If you took the task seriously, you undoubtedly struggled as you moved closer to number 1. Examine your list and note what you value and most importantly what your priority list says about you as a person. You might want to keep such thoughts in mind as you go on to the next exercise, telling the story of your life to another person.

Describing your life to another person is a simple but extremely useful exercise for it, too, focuses your attention on those events, people and relationships you consider most important. It is a process that can further clarify the characteristics you consider a part of your identity. Ideally the best person to tell your life story would be a stranger or someone who knows little of your history. However, you may not have such an opportunity and may choose a friend.

Many will find the exercise to be intimidating, peppered with uncertainty as to what to say. Good. You will be learning about your self. You will be beginning the conversation that will sensitize you to those actions and events you believe to be the most significant. Even tragic events (My mother died last year, I divorced in 1990, I never completed my education) can reveal what you value (Family is very important to me, I want to share my life with someone, I feel knowledge is critical to my well-being). There is no right picture. It is simply your picture—your unique story. To say it out loud is the beginning of the process of developing an answer to the questions "Who are you?" and "What do you stand for?"

Once you have chosen a partner for the exercise, share the following request:

> "I would like you to listen to me, uninterrupted, for four minutes. During that time I will tell you the story of my life. I would like to give me your complete attention but *without spoken words, prompts, or judgment.* When I have completed my story, I would like to reverse the process and hear you speak of your life for four minutes."

If this first step is too audacious for you or you do not feel you have a friend in whom you can confide, set a timer and talk to yourself. Be sure to suspend judgment as much as you can. If you are brave you may even tape record your story to hear at a later time.

The next and last exercise for this chapter is to set up a structure. Structure comes in many forms. In the world of rehabilitation, structure takes the form of appointments, expectations (goals) and practice established immediately after assessment. In business, a "corporate culture" and training are first steps implemented for success. In administration, by-laws, business plans, and yearly projections are integral to the field. In the world of nations we begin with a constitution and a set of laws. In each case one must set up an atmosphere that makes the projected change likely. In each case it is important to self-impose a set of rules that encourage function and change—be that physical improvement, financial success, growth or national well-being.

Growth on a personal basis can be very difficult. But let us start small. Let us set up a personal structure that encourages growth by recommitting to the affirmation in chapter 1 by placing it in a setting where it can been seen every day.

"I commit myself to take care of myself for the sake of myself, my family, my friends, my community and my country."

Such a commitment rests on the assumptions that healthy, strong individuals make for stronger relationships, friendships, and nations. It rests on the assumption that the kindest thing one can do for others is create personal well-being that, in turn, is likely to foster kindness and generosity to others. It is not selfish to develop strong character. It will ultimately mean self-respect for oneself and contribution to family, friends, community and nation.

This book is about character, well-being, development and growth. It is based on an assumption that we are capable of gaining increased control of our well-being by thoughtfully structuring our experiences and reconceptualizing our destructive beliefs.

It is my contention that identifying and improving one's strength of character is a worthy overt goal. Instead of passively allowing our personal qualities to evolve, I believe it is valuable to define one's character and then to proactively and deliberately pursue a strengthening of character.

Chapter 3

TAKING CHARGE

ISSUES of morality and character are not always clear. Consider a recent story in the "Washington Post" Magazine. Writing of her father, Irina Eremia Bragin describes a Rumanian career army officer who joined the Communist Party in the 1930's seeing it as the only opposition to the growing influence of the Nazi party. Soon, disillusioned by the corruption in communism, her father wrote a satirical political allegory, *Gulliver in the Land of Lies,* hoping to smuggle his work to France. His act of defiance, however, quickly turned to disaster as a friend betrayed his manuscript to the authorities. The resulting tragedy was that the bulk of his life was spent in prison, his career ruined and his family destroyed.

What makes this story both heroic and thought-provoking was the different perceptions of Irina's mother and father. While Irina's father listened to his principles, her mother had to live with the consequences. She had protested vehemently to his "self-destructive course." Her passion was not the future of her country but the welfare of her family. Devastated by her husband's actions and his imprisonment and fearful for her family's safety, she escaped from Romania and immigrated to the United States where her perseverance resulted in health and safety for her children.

Who's right? A man listening to idealistic notions which did not allow him to continue driving "in my limousine past long lines of desperate, starving people, endlessly waiting at stores whose shelves were bare" or to a woman who wished only to save her children from a life of persecution and hardship? Whose choice is correct—the idealistic or the pragmatic? Such questions are not easily answered.

Similar questions were raised in my mind with the recent passing of the Human Rights activist Reverend Maurice McCrackin—often called the "conscience of Cincinnati." Mac, as he liked to be called, lived to be 92 and died in a nursing home. As mentally sharp as ever up to his death, Mac stirred the sensitivities of local citizens by "walking his talk." Reviled and honored, dismissed as a nut, praised as a saint, Mac consistently gave the same message throughout his life—standing up, speaking out, willing to put his beliefs, his body, his reputation on the line—willing to consort with the incarcerated and the outcast. Inspired by Jesus Christ, Gandhi, Martin Luther King and Dorothy Day, he was repeatedly jailed, where he went on hunger strikes in protest of those acts which violated the principles he saw as basic to justice. His lack of cooperation with the courts and government tax system brought him into conflict with his church's policy and eventually resulting in his removal from the ministry of the Presbyterian church.[12] He, too, had to answer hard questions—questions which probably did not initially lead to clear answers.

In this book I have asked each of you to commit to taking care of yourself first, which I believe, in the long run, provides the most benefit to both yourself and others. How would such a recommendation be valuable in the face of difficult moral and ethical questions faced by the parents of Irina Eremia Bragin or by Reverend McCrackin? Was Irina's father putting his own idealistic needs before his family? And her mother? Was she taking care of her own needs by protecting her family? How does the question of character fit into the picture?

Challenging decisions evoking questions of character are not just faced in the drama of the world stage. Everyone must chose between the practical and the idealistic, the romantic and the pragmatic. The question of placing yourself first was put to the test most dramatically with a patient I saw many years ago. My patient's 20 year-old daughter had given birth to five children fathered by five different men. What made the situation more exasperating was that the daughter abandoned each child to her mother and continued her promiscuous ways. Further complicating this situation was the control that the daughter had over her mother—control and intimidation through violence. If my patient did not accommodate to the daughter's wishes, she would brutally beat her mother.

The above situation obviously calls for the assistance of the police and that was the first order of business. But, like most situations of this nature, the circumstances were more complex. The mother had previously called the police, but only as a last resort. My patient believed that it was necessary to put the needs of her grandchildren ahead of her own. To do otherwise appeared to be selfish and cruel. She could not see that by allowing her daughter's wishes to dominate her own, everyone suffered, even her grandchildren. In therapy she learned the importance of standing up for her own rights and to say no to her daughter. Such action took courage for a woman who had been subjugated by others all of her life. This patient was fortunate. After an additional attack and an immediate call to the police, the daughter understood that her mother was no longer going to appease her. She understood that additional children would be her responsibility and she proceeded to have her tubes tied. The patient learned the importance of caring for her own needs which, in turn, presented a different model of strength to both her daughter and grandchildren.

In each of these three widely divergent examples, we see a person facing an agonizing decision—Irina's father's decision to stand up for his ideals and face imprisonment and the knowledge that he was jeopardinzing his family or allow his conscience to suffer watching an unjust and cruel system of government; Irina's mother's choice between leaving the husband she loved and starting a new life with children in an unknown land or watching her children suffer under cruel and harsh conditions; Reverend McCrackin, a man who felt strongly that he should model himself after Jesus, who had to choose between taking positions which could and did bring harsh criticism from his parent church or follow what his conscience told him was right; my patient's choice between standing up to her daughter and putting her rights and needs first while risking harm or avoiding potential harm to herself and her grandchildren by continuing to act submissively. Not only are these decisions difficult but each alternative may have additional complications and ramifications. So is the experience of life. Taking care of yourself first often means facing difficult choices.

Taking care of yourself first sounds so selfish. Isn't it merely giving permission to be self-indulgent? Aren't self-indulgent people taking care of themselves first? What about people with addictions? Womanizers? Alcoholics? Drug Addicts? Work Addicts? Aren't these people caring for their own needs before the needs of others? They are—in the sense of taking care of their neurosis, their self-defeating behaviors. They are not taking care of themselves in the sense of what is good and right for their long-term well-being. They are out of control, controlled by external conditions, events beyond their command. I ask that you consider taking care of yourself from a different vantage point. I ask that you attend not to immediate gratification but to issues of long-term goals, strengthening of character, planning ahead and putting balance in your life. Taking care of yourself first with these criteria in mind constitutes the difference between acting with maturity versus acting with impulsiveness, self-centeredness and indulgence.

The behaviors of the addicted, the self-centered, the selfish are often motivated by fear and avoidance of looking too closely at personal feelings. The majority of those addicted to alcohol, drugs, work, power, status and attention are avoiding internal examination. Daily obsessions with short-term rewards cover up feelings of insecurity, isolation and loneliness. Such actions obscure feelings of hurt and fear of humiliation but sorrowfully result in an unnecessary shallowness—in lives lived far below their potential. Those courageous enough to face their inner demons can not only achieve more for themselves, but in the long run for others. Caring for oneself can truly be the first healthy step in caring for those around you.

Take the behaviors of the great leaders of our time: Mahatma Gandhi, Martin Luther King, Nelson Mandela and Mother Teresa. Considered from the point of view of what they gave to others, it would seem that they did not take care of themselves first. And close examination of each of their lives would reveal flaws, indiscretions, errors in judgment. But each also stands out because of his or her resolute attention to personal character, planning and balance. Each gave considerable thought to identity, purpose, issues of goodness and justice, and balance in their personal life. Their personal self-discipline included introspective time and time devoted to self-care (Mandela was unfailing in his exercise regimen while in prison; Gandhi adamant in taking time to spinning thread; Mother Teresa and Martin Luther King unwavering in their devotion to prayer). Each would not have given so significantly to those around them, to their community, to humanity, if they had not achieved a level of personal balance, given thought to long-term goals and devoted time to reflection, meditation or prayer. My intent is not to elevate each of us to the level of these world figures but to point out the value in giving ourselves permission, even insistence, in taking care of long-term goals, character building and personal needs.

Such recommendations are analogous to the instructions given by the airline personnel that, in an emergency, we place the oxygen mask over our own mouth before we tend to our children. If we place the mask on our child first and pass out from lack of oxygen, we can be of no benefit to our child. Whereas, if we place the mask over our own mouth first, we can revive a child who has momentarily passed out and later carry him or her to safety. What may initially strike us as selfish turns out to be smart, intelligent and beneficial to those under our care. So too with taking care of our personal needs. Not only are such acts wise but, in the long run, they benefit those around us.

There is another most critical reason for adamantly choosing to take care of ourselves first. It is that our personal thoughts and behaviors are under our control and no one else's. Consider again the lives of individuals consumed by addictive behaviors or whose lives are focused on status, power, class, wealth or material gain. When we examine their lives we are immediately struck by their lack of control, their inability to direct their own destiny. When we contrast them with others of greater maturity, we are struck with the ability of the latter to direct their own lives. It is the attention to those measures, which are under our personal control, such as character and adherence to principle that distinguish the truly successful. Success, in this light, stems from internal not external measures. Success from within has greater strength and durability. It is within everyone's reach.

Return again to the lives of the famous world figures I have alluded to. Were their lives without stress, anguish, hardship? Of course not. But each survived and grew in the face of adversity for having attended to their personal sense of identity, principle and character. It was by careful and extensive introspection that each gathered strength *before* life's trials that allowed them to endure and grow during these life's trials.

Clarifying one's values and principles provides a framework into which life's difficult decisions can be made with less pain, for knowledge of personal character and principle, itself, acts as a guide.

Knowing what you stand for and what your principles are can provide you with confidence. You are the person making the decision. You are the one who is facing up to the responsibility. You are the one who is being consistent. These internal decisions are not primarily contingent upon external factors. As such they provide immediate feedback confirming your identity—feedback which is the food of confidence.

Confidence is a state of mind, a perspective about oneself and one's ability to maneuver in the world. It is built on references to the past—those memories we believe to be relevant to the present and the future. When our mind is clear as to "who we are," we have boxes in our head to place our actions. "Yes, that was a kind thing to do—I am a kind person." "Yes, I did solve that difficult problem in a fair fashion—that's who I am." When we place our actions in the clearly labeled boxes that define who we are, we build our confidence.

Insecurity is exacerbated by the lack of definition regarding "who we are," what we stand for—the absence of boxes. Acts of kindness, generosity and the variety of decent behaviors can all too easily be considered exceptions to the rule, idiosyncratic, and germane to the circumstance, not to the individual. Such a process diminishes our confidence and builds our insecurity by allowing our worth to be based on external measures. Such perceptions contribute to feelings of poor self-worth and nurture distortions of reality.

Having a well-defined perception of your personal identity does not provide motivation in and of itself. Biology, interest, mood, consequences and other factors obviously play a major role. But character contributes guidelines, direction and energy. It is a basic building block upon which other influences are placed.

Using character as a measuring stick is more basic than external measures. Character asks more fundamental questions. Character deals with the "rightness" of an act. And character can provide comfort even when a decision results in suffering or pain.

The questions asked from character are often difficult ones: Do I cut corners, cheat, pilfer when it suits me? Do I backbite my boss, my competition, my friends in order to elevate my status? Do I act one way with one set of friends and entirely different with others? Do I treat one group of humans with less respect, fairness and justice than my own group? Am I acting responsibly in regard to my spouse, children, parents, family, friends, community and nation?

Such questions can bring uncomfortable responses—a discomfort that can initiate action. Such questions can create the dissonance that inspires the action which bring behavior back in line with character. Questions of character deal with honesty, integrity, fairness, trust, justice, kindness and other qualities that have more to do with goodness than advantage.

Actions taken in support of character need not mean self-sacrifice. The rewards simply are different, and in the greater picture, more substantive. Actions taken consistent with character provide long-term benefit. They have inherent worth which fits comfortably into the mind, body and the soul.

Listen to the words of an elderly, toil-worn black woman painfully traversing her four-mile walk in the tenth month of the Montgomery bus boycott. When a passerby sympathetically inquired if her feet were tired, she answered simply, "Yes, friend, my feet is tired, but my soul is rested."—a reply that was to become the boycotters' watchword. Actions consistent with good character feel wonderful.

Ponder the alternative to living a life of good character and principle. Small and large acts of dishonesty, deceit or cruelty sometimes provide short-term feelings of superiority, revenge, or power but nurture subsequent feelings of defensiveness, paranoia, and fear. The winning of a single battle leaves more battles to be fought, more enemies and more worries concerning one's ability to win the next engagement. No such negative consequences appear when attention is paid to measuring success by the yardstick of personal character.

Consider the comfort to the mind, body and soul when acts are done consistent with what you believe to be your true identity. Self-recriminations, body tensions and spiritual doubts are fewer. And, in the long run, conflict with our fellow men and women is likely to be less as well.

The dichotomy between right and wrong, long and short-term consequences, however, is not always clear. Life is difficult and decisions complicated. Our fears and insecurities are real and we can't control the actions of others. We may act in what we consider to be a kind, trusting, and fair fashion, only to find others misperceiving our actions and justice seemingly turned on its head. To accept the fact that such is the nature of the world is also a matter of character. It is an understanding and maturity which stands at a higher level than many of the other qualities of goodness, for it allows the continuation of character. To accept that unfairness, injustice and suffering are a part of our existence is to open the door to perseverance and tolerance, further bolstering our character.

Difficult and complicated questions are more easily resolved when our own principles are clear—principles which grow out of identity, character and goodness. The "rules" are out there, explicitly stated. "This action must be consistent with my character, who I am and what I stand for. I promised myself that I would be honest and these are the honest actions I need to take right now." A commitment has been made.

The internal dialog is different when character is poorly defined. The dialog becomes more focused on external events and actions tend to be guided by the environment—producing short-term gain and long-term problems.

Let's return to the decisions made by the players in the stories told at the beginning of the chapter. Irina's father spent considerable time in prison. A life lost? Not according to him. He felt justified in his sacrifice and could even write the following from his prison cell:

> *"I don't care about the wind and the snowstorm, or the cold that penetrates deep into the bone. Never in my life have I felt more free. My spirit is intact! I learned to sing without sound and to write without paper. Despite everything, man remains the most marvelous, the most accomplished creature wrought by nature!"* [13]

Irina's father—a life marked by courage and determination. And what of Irina's mother? She too felt vindicated by her actions. Her children grew to be successful in life, comforted and guided by their mother's strength. And what of Rev. McCrackin? His life impacted literally thousands of individuals through simple acts of kindness. And he too felt an inner serenity. Mac said, "I never had more peace of mind than when I was in jail because I believed in what I was doing and I had followed through."[14] Martin Luther King Jr., when incarcerated in the Birmingham city jail, reported similar thoughts.

And last, my patient—what became of her? She too redirected her life, devoting time to her grandchildren and herself. Free from the burden of fear, she found new ways to give and receive.

I leave it to others to argue the merits of each choice. The critical factor is not the definitive answer as to what is absolutely right or wrong. The critical fact is that the questions were faced, not avoided. The decisions were made by asking hard questions and looking inward.

As we examine these lives, however, we can observe that the answers to difficult questions were probably easier for those who had already faced questions of personal identity, values and purpose. For those who had already decided that it was important to put their own principles first, life's demands were just a little bit easier, a little less painful. For these people have a history of measuring their lives by a standard of behavior under their control. These people have guidelines of behavior which influence their decisions, giving stability and comfort during the stresses of their lives.

Chapter 3 has promoted the importance of prioritizing your energy and your behaviors, specifically recommending that you care for yourself first.

Benjamin Franklin made up a code of conduct, a code that also provided a measure of the man. Franklin was said to have listed twelve personal behaviors he felt were important enough to measure each day and by their existence, helped him to live a life he considered worthy. I could in no way outdo the recommendations of Benjamin Franklin and therefore commend to you a similar exercise. Let us, however, expand on Franklin's good recommendations by choosing not only conduct of which we can be proud but also by providing a working definition of each, so the behavior is clearly specified. Completing this exercise will help reveal those behaviors you believe both to be important and to be part of your make-up—a good early step in identifying your character.

I have provided an example of a code of conduct. Please review it and fill out your own code on the following page.

Code of Conduct—Example

I will be:

Honest: I am honest when I follow the "Golden Rule."

Good Humored: I am good humored when I put events in perspective.

Optimistic: I am optimistic when I have confidence in the future.

Assertive: I am assertive when I speak up in spite of my fears.

Passionate: I am passionate when I speak honestly to my feelings.

Grateful: I am grateful when I attend to the moment and to my good fortune.

Generous: I am generous when I think of the needs of others.

Responsible: I am responsible when I follow my stated mission.

Listener: I am a good listener when I can accurately describe the perception of others.

Code of Conduct—Your Own Personal Code

1.

2.

3.

4.

5.

6.

7.

8.

9.

10.

I commit myself to take care of myself for the sake of myself, my family, my friends, my community and my country.

Chapter 4

THE CHALLENGES WE FACE

THE symptoms are devastating—loss of sleep, irritability, vague general pains, loss of sexual drive, energy, and the ability to concentrate. The numbers are incredible. Never before have so many Americans been "infected." Experts like Drs. Martin Seligman and Terrence Real tell us that each generation "contracts" this illness at an earlier age and that severity of its occurrence has increased. In spite of its ubiquity, however, no public outcry has occurred. No national drive to eradicate its occurrence like efforts for cancer, heart disease, and diabetes has been launched. And yet, it effects virtually every American family. What is this blight on the landscape? Depression, of course.

The enormous increase in depression is even more striking when we examine the female to male ratio. Consistently, through a multitude of studies and surveys, the incidence of depression has been found to occur in women twice as often as men. This curious finding has been the subject of extensive study and analysis with a wide range of hypotheses ranging from women being willing to respond more openly to questions concerning depression, more willing to visit therapists, subject to more stress while earning less money, and to having more gender role pressure. Each hypothesis, respectively, has been found wanting. The ratio of two-to-one is constant in both public and anonymous conditions, in door-to-door surveys and when women and men are matched for financial status and employment. Women who have both work and home responsibilities are found to be less depressed on average than women who are not employed, making the likelihood of sex role pressure less plausible as the primary reason for the contrast.[15]

The disparity between the sexes is understandable, however, when we read the work of psychotherapist Terrence Real. In an illuminating analysis, Real points out that women are enculturated to suppress their voice, inhibit their *behaviors* and *internalize* blame for the difficulties in their lives. The suppression of action and subsequent rumination promotes the occurrence of depression. Taught to inhibit their real potential in their quest to establish harmonious relationships, women pay an enormous price in the form of additional depression.

Men, on the other hand, are enculturated to inhibit their *emotions* and are more prone to *externalize* blame and act out during periods of frustration. Acting out and externalizing blame serves to reduce depression. Whereas women, as a group, are more prone to suppress their behaviors, men are more likely to suppress their feelings. Carried to a fine art, one psychologist[16] believes that nearly 80% of men suffer a mild-to-severe form of alexithymia—the psychiatric term for the inability to be in touch with one's own emotions. Traditional masculine training places emphasizes upon self-worth being achieved through performance. In the more competitive male world, expression of emotion permits vulnerability that can endanger performance. Men protect themselves by becoming so proficient at hiding their emotions that they manage to bury them from themselves. The differences in response to life's stresses (women internalizing and suppressing their potential and men externalizing and acting out) between the genders are then attributed to the discrepancy in the occurrence of depression.

However, as Real points out, this is only a part of the picture. For while men's tendency to act out during life's frustrations staves off the feelings of depression, such behavior does not actually resolve the discomfort. The feelings are there but pushed down. In their stead are behaviors that are too often acted out in a dysfunctional fashion—drinking, drug use, excessive work, etc. In these areas men far outnumber women. When these numbers are tallied along with figures concerning depression, the inequity between the sexes disappears. In other words, the incidence of depression in the United States is increasing and occurring at a younger and younger age. And when we include the neurotic acting out of men in our statistic analysis, these increases are true equally for men and women.[17]

A society showing increasing incidence of depression is not healthy. But depression is the outer expression of some additional worrisome trends. A major component of the increase in the national incidence of depression stems from an increase in isolation, loneliness and lack of meaningful connections. Each trend emerges from social changes of our times. Consider the following:

- "In 1945, about 85 % of all Americans lived in extended families. In the 1990's roughly 3% do."[18]
- "In 1993, 27 percent of children under age eighteen lived with one parent, up from 12 percent in 1970."[19]

- "...only 35 percent of American families sit down around a table and eat at least one meal together every day."[20]
- "In 1995, according to the Census Bureau, one in four Americans over eighteen (about 44 million) had never married, up from one in six in 1970. At any given time, about half the adult Americans were not married. In 1993, 23.6 million adults lived alone, up 15 percent since 1985."[21]
- "More than 40 percent of children aged 6-11 have televisions in their bedroom to watch on their own."[22]
- "By the year 2010, 31 million Americans will be living alone."[23]

Living alone doesn't necessarily mean feeling lonely. But there are many indications that ties and bonds present in previous generations have been eliminated or greatly reduced. This is reflected in the response Dr. Dean Ornish reports when he asked the following series of questions during speaking engagements:

"How many can say yes to all 4 of the following:

1. That you live in the same neighborhood that you were born and raised in and that most of your neighbors are still there.
2. That you've been working in the same job for 10 years and that most of your co-workers are still there.
3. That you've attend the same church or synagogue for 10 years and most of the same congregants are still there.
4. That you have an extended family that is within driving distance of you."

Ornish reports that in speaking to audiences of 3,000, he often will have only roughly 10 to 20 people raise their hands giving affirmation to all four questions.[24] Such responses are only one indication of how mobility has radically changed the nature of our relationships in the past seventy years.

The traditional, old-world extended family—two or three generations living together—effectively disappeared after World War II and has now been further modified by the enormous increase in the employment patterns of American women. The new standard in the American family is one in which both the husband and wife work. In 1992, 46 percent of all married couples had both partners employed, up from one-third in 1972. The figures are even more striking when we examine households with children under six years of age. In 1960, 19 percent of married women in such households were in the workforce while that number hovered around 65 percent in 1995.[25]

While such figures could be interpreted as a reflection of major gains in opportunities for women, it also means that parents and children are seeing less of each other. According to the Parent Teacher Association, there are an estimated 7 million latch-key children between the ages of five and thirteen who care for themselves after school until a parent comes home from work. Only half of the 66 million American children live in traditional two-parent families.[26]

Work demands are affecting more than just child-parent relationships. Psychologists specializing in sexual problems have reported an enormous increase in sexual dysfunction attributed to just plain exhaustion. The demands of work and parenting are leaving little time or energy for intimacy.

The separation of children from mothers, fathers, grandparents, uncles, aunts, and cousins diminishes cultural practices of rites of passage and initiation ceremonies—practice that previously provided children and adolescents structure, safety and guidance into the early stages of adulthood. Such losses are significant. Mother Teresa was aware of the consequences when she "was said to have observed that Americans were poorer than the people of India for Americans suffered the pains of loneliness."[27]

In addition to the fact that more Americans are living alone, there are indications that shared lives aren't necessarily connected. Connected lives refers to more than the sharing of time, but the sharing of feelings, vulnerabilities, intimacies, common memories and hopes. Connected lives share concerns and a sense of responsibility for the other person. Connectedness cannot be measured simply by the quantity of time spent together although lives devoted to excessive work may leave little time to experience connectedness. Connected refers to the quality of relationships. The stresses of our times has exerted enormous pressure on the quality of our lives—pressure in the form of work, adjustments to rapidly changing technologies, and social changes. Many of these pressures have left us with less time to share but, more importantly, with an empty feeling even when we are with others.

The lack of connectedness shows up in both obvious and subtle ways. The obvious is in the form of a high divorce rate. Less obvious are obsessive work habits which make connecting with friends and family difficult; in the need to take along work or call the office when going on vacation; in the recent interest in massage therapy, "healing touch" and books on spirituality. Even the rapid rise of Alternative Medicine with its emphasis upon listening, stems in part, from a dissatisfaction with the distant impersonal nature of modern medicine. In each example there is evidence of a need to connect with another human being.

Increasingly, interest in real relationships has been replaced to a large degree by television and celebrities. It is marvelous that Oprah Winfry is personable and Jerry

Seinfield makes us laugh, but as others have noted, Oprah can't hold my hand or give me a hug during troubled times. Jerry's not there to cheer me up when I've suffered a loss. And even worse, Oprah and Jerry and all the other celebrities may have lured me into the numbing habit of watching more television than I intended to—a habit which replaces the time I could have spent doing meaningful activities with the real people in my life—activities which could contribute to intimacy, closeness and connectedness. Not every moment of our lives needs to be devoted to meaningful activities, but with a culture filled with work pressures and superficial acquaintances, we can ill afford 20 or more hours per week devoted to people who are not our real friends and relatives.

Social change can be like a frog in a pot—the heat is turned up so gradually that it is not noticed. Only when we compare the current condition to the past is the extent of the change recognized as substantial. Family settings in which conversation was the primary entertainment occurred often sixty years ago and can still be found today, just not with the same frequency. Neighborhoods still exist where families share in each other's lives, just not as often. Neighborhoods still exist where families know the names and details of their merchant's lives, but they are rare. And parents continue to tell stories and teach character lessons, when they have time.

If we look around America today with the high rate of divorce and job insecurity and the number of children reared in single parent households, the occurrence of empty feelings and the need for stability has never been greater. The culture of the 1940's and 50's was far from perfect and certainly not glamorous. It had its own challenges. But we should also be aware that progress in the past sixty years has brought considerable baggage.

The societal changes that leave people more alone are hard on physical health as well as relationships. Americans who are alone are more likely to pay in the form of disease, illness and premature death. Dr. Dean Ornish reports that extensive studies have shown that people who feel lonely and isolated are three to five more times likely to have a premature death.[28]

Ornish, as you may recall, is the cardiologist who directed clinical research, demonstrating for the first time that comprehensive lifestyle changes can begin to reverse even severe coronary heart disease, without drugs or surgery. In his latest book, *Love and Survival*, he extensively reviews research concerning loneliness, cardiac disease and survival. Consistently, a variety of studies conducted in countries around the world demonstrate that loneliness is a primary contributor to heart disease and poor health. Consider the following:

- *"Studies of long-lived people [as opposed to those who die young] show that working more than 40 hours a week [particularly if your work isn't meaningful to you], experiencing loneliness on a regular basis, and getting less than eight hours of sleep on average correlate to rapid aging and premature death."* [29]

- *"Women who actually had many social contacts but reported feeling lonely [those who couldn't let the love in] had a 2.4 times greater risk of developing hormone-related cancers including uterine, breast, and ovarian than those who felt connected. Women who actually did have fewer social contacts and also felt isolated had five times the risk of dying from these cancers."* [30]

- *Patients who underwent open-heart surgery and who lacked regular participation in organized social groups were found to have a fourfold increased risk of dying six months after surgery.* [31]

Although not well acknowledged in much of the medical community, the link between loneliness and diminished health is well documented in the research literature.

If loneliness and isolation can increase depression and ill-health, then the opposite of loneliness—social contact, support groups and the like—must be the remedy. Indeed there is evidence to support such a proposition. The often-cited research of David Spiegel at Stanford Medical School is one such example. In an attempt to prove that psychological and social factors did *not* prolong life in breast cancer patients, Dr. Spiegel randomly assigned women with metastatic breast cancer to one of two groups, with both groups receiving conventional medical care such as chemotherapy, radiation, medication and surgery. Beyond this treatment, one group of women met for 90 minutes each week for a year to regularly discuss their fears and the reactions of friends and to express their feelings concerning dying and disfigurement. What Spiegel found astounded him. Five years following treatment, the women who had the opportunity to share their inner concerns not only fared better but they lived twice as long as the group of women who did not participate in the support group. In the ensuing years since Dr. Spiegel's 1989 research, investigators have continued to find a similar relationship between survival and supports groups.

If you don't have heart disease or a chronic disease, the issue of loneliness as a causative factor for these problems may not seem relevant to your life. But loneliness, lack of connectedness and depression does more than affect our health. It influences the quality of our lives. These trends can harm us individually, harm our community and harm our nation.

CHARACTER AS REMEDY

How do men and women make sure they are not harmed by the influences that contribute to depression? How do we avoid loneliness and fill our lives with closeness and intimacy?

The answers to these questions are best viewed from a new paradigm—a perspective that rejects the *traditional* views of masculinity and femininity. To understand the new perspective, it is useful to characterize the traditional viewpoints.

From an early age girls are measured by their beauty and, not long after, by dependence. Significant progress has been made in the past half-century to counter these influences, but these pressures remain a powerful forces in molding the behavior of the American female. The extraordinary incidence of eating disorders, (only present in cultures with an obsession with thinness); the fanciful images of marriage emanating from the entertainment and bridal industries; and the decline in academic achievement as girls reach junior high school, attest to the continuing effect of society's pressures for women to be beautiful and dependent.

Psychologist I.K. Broverman conducted a study that illustrates the dilemma faced by young women in late 20th century America. Men and women were asked to check off adjectives they believed to be characteristics representative of healthy men, healthy women, and healthy adults. Participants described healthy men and healthy adults similarly— as independent, active and logical. Healthy women, on the other hand, were described as passive, dependent and illogical. In other words, it was impossible to be both a healthy woman and a healthy adult.

If young women revolt against the pressures to measure their worth by beauty and dependence, they risk the sanctions of their peers. If they adopt the external standards of beauty and dependency, women gain the short-term benefits of adoration, attention and affiliation but, in the long-term, accept a standard that is fragile and shallow.

Men labor under a different burden. For the traditional male, success is achieved by external accomplishments— winning in sports, business, or power. However, external accomplishments don't necessarily bring internal well-being. The famous baseball player, Ty Cobb, is a prime example. Cobb was the greatest major league player of his time. Ferociously competitive, Cobb would do anything to win and to elevate his personal statistics. If winning meant flying into a base with sharp spikes high, or tormenting, beating-up or baiting an opposing player, so be it. Vehemently prejudiced, Cobb battled nearly everyone. His own teammates, at various times, refused to play with him in spite of the fact that his combativeness and talents would likely lead to victory. At the end of his playing career, during which he set dozens of records including the highest life-time average in major league history, he left baseball and returned to his small hometown in Georgia. Estranged from family and former teammates, Cobb lived out the rest of his life desolate, bitter and alone. He won at the game of baseball but lost at the game of life.

Ty Cobb illustrates the case made by psychotherapist Terrence Real, that many men become addicted to external success in order to avoid dealing with their emotions. Encouraged by an ethos that promotes external success as a measure of masculinity, many men will go to almost any lengths to win and to avoid vulnerability. In the process, they greatly reduce their potential for real intimacy, for vulnerability is the gateway to intimacy.

Accepting the standards of traditional masculinity and femininity in the context of a society that has become progressively isolated is dangerous. For the traditional man, the suppression of feelings reduces the likelihood of real intimacy and connectedness. Without the safety net of the relatively stable, multigenerational family and a community of lifelong friends that were more prevalent in the past, he is left in a position of isolation. For the traditional woman who adopts society's standards of beauty and dependence, she risks being a real person. She risks even knowing what she is capable of doing. Without the support of stable and extended family and long-term friendships, the danger of feeling alone and depressed is increased and her self-worth is left up to external judgements.

For both men and women, the healthy alternative is to turn away from traditional measures of masculinity and femininity and create standards that promote well-being, intimacy, love, and authenticity. Men can voice their feelings, work toward win-win answers, and be willing to be vulnerable. Women can speak their voices, express their independence and their ambitions. Such acts move past disingenuous outward appearance and toward honest and internal standards. They can move toward authenticity and lay the groundwork for closeness, intimacy and friendship.

Another perspective regarding questions of depression and loneliness can be found in research concerning parenting styles. Some children seem to be protected from the harmful influences of our society. Psychologists have long been interested in discovering what parenting style is most effective in producing such individuals. Two broad dimensions have emerged—affection/acceptance and parental control strategies.

As you might expect, critical, unaccepting, undemanding parents tend to have children who, by their teen-age years, have a variety of problems, including delinquency and chemical dependency. Authoritarian parents have children who are socially inadequate and lacking in confidence. Indulgent parents tend to have children who are dependent, impulsive and not responsible. The fourth combination, parents who are high in acceptance but also high in control, tend to have children who are independent, socially responsible and confident. In other words, the parents who are strict but loving are most likely to be giving the message, "We love you, but you must do as we say."[32] These parents tend to expect a great deal of their children, give clear messages concerning what they expect and make their love evident. They have children who, on the whole, tend to be well-adjusted.

As with so many recommendations concerning children, the process of parenting can also serve as a good model for adults. If we are interested in becoming independent, socially responsible and confident, we must create clear, high personal standards coupled with compassion and loving acceptance for ourselves.

In this analogy the "strict parent", high in control, sets high personal standards which expect the best of qualities, and are precisely defined and frequently stated. At the same time we need compassion and love. The message, "We love you, but you must do as we say" can translate to the belief that "I measure myself by internally defined high standards and accept myself with my flaws and inadequacies." Such a belief, if held to, is likely to result in an independent, confident and responsible person with a clearly defined identity.

Some would argue that the difficulties in our society stem not from personal inadequacies but from structural problems—a government too unresponsive or too intrusive, politicians who are too liberal or too conservative, a legal system that is too permissive or too punitive, schools that are too lax, hospitals that don't care, insurance companies and businesses that are too profit-oriented. I take a different point of view. Governments, legal systems, schools, hospitals, insurance and businesses are made up of people like you and me. Many are good and kind. However, given a culture that measures worth by external standards, it is all too easy to attend to immediate interest—promotions, material acquisitions, short-term advantages, status, and intolerance of differences. Such short-term attitudes lend themselves more easily to competition than cooperation, and to exclusiveness and prejudice than to inclusiveness and tolerance. When such attitudes become part of the people who fill our institutions, then the institutions themselves express these characteristics.

If our society is to make significant progress that includes the social needs of our families, communities and our nation, we will need a new paradigm. The new institutions must be filled with people attuned to long-term values—values that include both personal welfare and the welfare of family, friends, community and nation. If our politicians, lawyers, judges, teachers, medical personnel, insurance executives, businessmen and women, and each of us abide by high personal standards, we will successfully stave off the forces leading to loneliness and depression and instead create a society valued for its trust and community.

I commit myself to take care of myself for the sake of myself, my family, my friends, my community and my country.

Chapter 5

BELIEFS: THE FOUNDATION OF

CHARACTER

TAKING four years and using airplanes between continents, Steven Newman literally walked around the world. Sheila M. had already seen 105 doctors by documentation when I first saw her in 1985. Harry S. had been to emergency rooms in Cincinnati, Ohio, over 100 times in the preceding year when I interviewed him in 1991. Wilber F. had 23 doctors and health care professionals treating him at the same time when I saw him in 1994.

David Koresh, self-proclaimed messenger of God, led his flock to a fiery and tragic death in 1993. Over 800 men, women and children, committed suicide following the "teachings" of self-anointed prophet, Jim Jones, in Guyana in 1978.

How did the horrible actions of Hermann Goring, Adolf Hitler, Joseph Goebbels, Saddam Hussein, and Idi Amin

come about? Or the extraordinary lives of Mother Teresa,
Albert Schweitzer, Martin Luther King, Mahatma Gandhi,
and Nelson Mandela?

In each and every case, for good, evil or self-destruction,
the actions of these people came about because of the beliefs they held. As Anthony Robbins[33] notes in his book,
Awaken the Giant Within,[34] beliefs have the power to create
and beliefs have the power to destroy. As Stephen Covey
writes in *The 7 Habits of Highly Effective People*,[35] ". . . All things
are created twice. There's a mental or first creation, and a
physical or second creation to all things."

It takes more than just a belief to achieve the outcomes
associated with each of the above individuals. Mental hospitals are filled with psychotics who believe they are the mes-
sengers of god, and no doubt, many thousands of pre-war
Germans believed in the superiority of the Aryan race. Beliefs were just a part of the equation. It also took the enormously persuasive powers of Jim Jones and Adolf Hitler
to attain the horrible consequences associated with these
men.

Persuasive abilities and personal habits aside, it is their
belief systems that stood as the critical and necessary ingre-
dient for their behavior. Without their beliefs, they would
not be the people they were and would not have behaved in
the manner that they did. Similarly, the great achievements
of Mahatma Gandhi, Nelson Mandela, Mother Teresa and
Albert Schweitzer also stand on the foundation of their belief system. We need not turn to famous and powerful people,
nor individuals with chronic health conditions, however, to
illustrate the importance of beliefs systems. Each and every
one of our actions is subject to the influence, directly or
indirectly, of our beliefs. Each and every part of our character
is based upon our beliefs. The surprising factor is that we pay
so little attention to either acknowledging or examining
them.

BELIEFS THAT HARM

Limiting Beliefs

Robert K. is an example of the harm created by a mistaken belief. To watch Robert move was in itself painful. His entire walk said, "I'm in pain, don't touch me." Even more than his pained expression and the tension evident in every step were his speed of movement. There was almost none. He moved so slowly that we had significant concerns as to whether he could participate in treatment. Our sessions required that the patient go from therapy to therapy and Robert arrived so late that his whole program began to be undermined.

Robert was in his late fifties and the subject of three cervical operations including a fusion. Like so many chronic pain patients he was depressed, but it was his tension and tightness that was most pronounced. The physical and occupational therapists noted that he could move his neck no more than a few centimeters without expressing intense pain—his neck and entire shoulder region were extremely hard from tension. Anyone observing Robert and knowing his cervical history could easily assume that substantial organic damage was present. They would have been only partially correct, however, and would have missed out on a most critical variable—his beliefs.

Robert did not have a family physician. He relied on his orthopedic surgeon for medical care, the same doctor who had performed his operations. It appeared that Robert's physician did not know how to further treat him after three surgeries and many narcotic prescriptions. Seeing his patient progressively deteriorate, he told Robert that if he moved too fast, his "spine would crumble." We didn't know if

Robert's recollection of his physician's statement was accurate, but we did know that he believed in its veracity. Anyone watching him move would be convinced of that. It was clear that Robert's incredibly slow movement was based on his pain and his strong belief that if he moved too fast, his spine would crumble. (More on Robert later on in the chapter)

Most beliefs are probably acquired as the result of an accumulation of data or "evidence." Some, however, appear to almost become imprinted, the result of a dramatic message occurring at a time when the listener was vulnerable. This is what apparently happens in many of the inappropriate "lessons of life" that we acquire as young children or in the extraordinary, but inappropriate perception, acquired by Robert. When the message learned is constructive ("I'm capable of doing many different tasks"), little harm is done and perhaps some good. But on other occasions, we may acquire negative and damaging beliefs ("My spine will crumble if I walk too fast" or "I'm a jerk at social gatherings"), which we accept as gospel. We have little awareness of the potential harm that beliefs can do to our lives.

"LABELING" BELIEFS

I once observed a patient in treatment acting very excited and happy. I went up to her and said, "My, you're ebullient this morning." Looking somewhat surprised, she said, "What's ebullient?" "Oh, ebullient means, full of energy, alive, excited and happy." Later on that same day I overheard a staff member asking my patient, "What got into you today?" "I'm ebullient," replied the patient. This little example represents a very temporary label, one that probably had a short-term effect. But what of other labels people give themselves—disabled, worthless, inadequate, stupid. Many of these labels

are strong and resistant to change. In the example above, a
label can be beneficial. Just as easily, a labeling belief can do
harm—great harm. Take the case of Amy S.:

> Amy was 42 years old and had a 20-year history
> of Ankylosing Spondylitis. Her spinal curvature
> was so severe that she was literally looking at her
> shoes and only with significant effort was able
> to make eye contact. She had undergone mul-
> tiple treatment procedures for pain relief, in-
> cluding epidural steroids and anesthetics as well
> as several attempts at maintaining an epidural
> narcotic catheter—all with no benefit. She re-
> ported substantial energy loss and fatigue and
> stated that she was unmotivated to do anything.
> Her only activity was getting up to eat once per
> day. She had recently been detoxified from her
> narcotic medication with inpatient treatment
> at a local hospital but said she was currently
> consuming a case of beer daily as an analgesic
> for her chronic pain. After some discussion she
> revealed that she had recently been arrested
> for driving while intoxicated (for which she was
> extremely embarrassed) and had been forced
> in seek treatment as a result.

Amy indicated that her pain was primarily in her back, radiating around her rib cage and occurred on a daily level. She
also noted secondary but very intense pain in her hips. Any
movement increased her pain, which was the reason for her
inactivity.

On the day of her evaluation, she walked with great difficulty, was reliant upon a cane and stated that the maximum
she could walk was one block. Her symptoms first appeared

when she was seventeen and become "official" a few years later. Shortly after her entrance into the office she produced a three page article describing Ankylosing Spondylitis. The article had been carried for many years and was tattered from use. She believed her diagnosis was degenerative and could not be reversed except by a very risky surgical procedure which had little chance of success.

Her personal life was further complicated by a bad marriage in which she now lived in the lower level of her house, rarely interacting with or even seeing her husband. Amy clearly had given up any hope of improving, believing (as one doctor had told her) that "she had to learn to live with her pain."

Upon formal admission to the rehabilitation program, Amy's physical examination revealed that her muscles were very tight and shortened from lack of use. They were also extremely sensitive to touch. Surprisingly, there was an *absence* of general signs of substantial "calcification" of the patient's back and radiographic imaging revealed only modest Ankylosis Spondolysis. There were, however, indications of severe myofascial pain syndrome (i.e. intense damage to the covering of the musculature). Myofascial pain syndrome differs enormously from Ankylosis Spondolysis in that it is quite reversible. The diagnosis that Amy had believed for over 20 years was false.

Believing that her condition meant a life of suffering and pain, Amy progressed into to a life of depression, withdrawal and substance dependence.

Beliefs can direct a life. The power of beliefs alone, should be enough for each of us to look at their origins. They may be based on information from an unreliable source, have been more true at another time than at the present, or be based on faulty information or interpretation of that information. A prominent characteristic of beliefs, however, is that right or wrong they are rarely questioned.

BELIEFS THAT HARM OTHERS

One of the most memorable failures in treatment was a frail, emaciated woman in her late fifties. She weighed less than 90 pounds and, quite frankly, had a very sour disposition. She came into the program with a long history of low back pain. We soon observed, however, that her cardiac condition which was aggravated by three packs of cigarettes daily and intense worry was much more threatening to her life. As she began the program she surprised us and made considerable progress. She took joy in her increased activity, found support from her fellow patients, and showed signs of reducing her anxiety and muscle tension. Unfortunately, all these gains were ended when we met the patient's husband. He had another agenda. He believed his wife to be disabled and demanded that we sign papers supporting his contention. We disputed his belief (which we suspected was supported by potential financial gain) and refused to sign the papers. He promptly escorted her wife out of the hospital against medical advice.

Interestingly, we have had numerous family members who believe their relatives are disabled and treat them accordingly. In a rehabilitation setting we view patients as having limitations but we work to increase their strengths. This difference in beliefs and expectations appears to be a critical element in the extraordinary gains commonly acquired in rehabilitation.

WHAT ARE BELIEFS AND

WHY DO WE HAVE THEM?

Webster's Third New International Dictionary defines a belief as "a state or habit of mind in which trust, confidence or reliance is placed in some person or thing." Anthony Robbins, succinctly defines it as "a state of certainty." No person is without beliefs and most rarely question them. Once established there appear to be internal mechanisms to support their existence and to deny opposing beliefs. Why do they exist in the first place? What is their purpose? Most simply, beliefs provide a set of internal guidelines by which we navigate our lives—generalizations concerning our experiences and our environment. If I believe a certain area of the city is dangerous, I avoid that section. If I believe that promptness is a virtue, I attempt to make my appointments on time. If I believe that I can never learn a particular skill, I am likely to avoid trying. In each case the belief provides a shorthand guide to be used in our quest of seeking pleasure and avoiding pain. We need not test every new circumstance but can use beliefs as a resource.

When used as an efficient means of processing new information, beliefs can be useful and beneficial. The difficulty arises, however, when we consider that beliefs can easily be faulty. Just a short time ago, the majority of Americans believed that smoking was harmless and even sexy. Incredibly, some people still do. Similarly, people saw little harm in consuming large quantities of fatty food and being very sedentary. Views change. What was usual in one decade may be incomprehensible the next. It is for exactly this reason that it is critical that we define our beliefs and examine their origins whenever possible.

Many beliefs begin when we are children and these beliefs, established at an early age, can be particularly resistant to change. This is very unfortunate when we realize that many of these early beliefs are based on faulty information. Numerous factors account for this situation. First, we are more apt to accept information uncritically. Most of us acquire the skill of critical thinking with age but its absence at an early age allows for more indiscriminate acceptance of information. Second, we are perhaps in the most dependent period of our lives and are thereby open to new beliefs received directly and indirectly from authority figures.

The youthful openness to new information, concepts and ideas is, of course, a valuable asset for an enormous amount of learning. The problem arises when beliefs are acquired during this period become the foundation for subsequent life decisions that are self-destructive.

Remember that beliefs are basically generalizations—generalizations in which the person has a significant degree of confidence and certainty. It is fine to generalize from one toy block to another toy block, noticing the similarity, from one car to another car, again noticing the similarity and so forth. Small errors in distinguishing between objects of this nature do little harm. The same cannot be said regarding the generalization from one behavior to another. If I have failed at this task once, should I generalize to the belief that I will regularly fail at this task or that I fail at all tasks?

In my clinical experience, I often encounter patients who walk with a cane and therefore state that they are disabled. Walking with a cane and using the label "disabled" are two separate matters. There can be no argument that a person walks with a cane—that is an observable fact. A disability is a generalization that, for most people, has considerable additional meaning. Generalizing from the observation "I walk with a cane" to "I am disabled" can be profoundly disempowering. It is important that we be as specific and objective as possible in considering any belief that has the potential to harm our view of ourselves or the world around us.

BELIEFS THAT BUILD: MEN AND WOMEN

WHO HAVE "WALKED THEIR TALK"

One of the most destructive personal beliefs involves believing that others are to blame for our discomfort and suffering. The act of blaming disempowers, the act of taking responsibility empowers. It is for this reason that each chapter of this book ends with the affirmation—"I commit myself to take care of myself for the sake of myself, my family, my friends and my community"—an affirmation that states personal responsibility. It is my belief that personal happiness can be enhanced by rational efforts, by systematic planning, practice and the cultivation of character. I believe that, as we examine the process by which individual and societal neuroses occur, we acquire the means to heal our own distress. I believe that the process begins and ultimately resides within ourselves. As we take responsibility for our own problems, our own thoughts, beliefs, attitudes and behaviors and ask whether we have done enough, or can do more, we then move forward. To blame others, before fully developing our own potential, is not only irresponsible but a formula for disaster.

Stephen Covey[36] suggests that we move from a "circle of concern" to a "circle of influence". He refers to the circle of concern as a focus on issues outside ourself—issues about which we can worry, fret and blame, but do little. By turning our focus instead to the development of our character, attending to our own issues, we gain greater control over areas that are truly accessible to change. In doing so we find that our ability to influence is actually increased. I strongly concur with his observations.

Perhaps no other man in the twentieth century more illustrates the power of personal influence than Mahatma Gandhi. This incredible human being, so small in physical stature, defied the great nation of Britain and was more instrumental than any other man in gaining India its independence. Through acts of personal sacrifice for the sake of his people and his country, his influence increased. His authority grew to the point where his followers were willing to risk injury, disfigurement and death because of their reverence and loyalty to the man and his mission. Possibly the most vivid example of the courage inspired by this remarkable leader was described by Webb Miller, the well-known correspondent of the United Press, who was on the scene when 2500 of Gandhi's followers confronted 400 Surat policemen under the command of six British officers. These men, followers of Gandhi philosophy of non-violent resistance, had been told "you must not resist, you must not even raise a hand to ward off a blow." Webb Miller described the proceedings:

> "In complete silence the Gandhi men drew up and halted a hundred yards from the stockade. A picked column advanced from the crowd, waded the ditches, and approached the barbed-wired stockade. "

Ordered to retreat they continued to advance:

> "Suddenly, " Miller reported, "at a word of command, scores of native policemen rushed upon the advancing marchers and rained blows on their heads with their steel-shod lathis. Not one of the marchers even raised a

arm to fend off the blows. They went down like ten-pins. From where I stood I heard the sickening whack of the clubs on unprotected skulls. The waiting crowd of marchers groaned and sucked in their breath in sympathetic pain at every blow. Those struck down fell sprawling, unconscious or writhing with fractured skulls or broken shoulders. The survivors, without breaking ranks, silently and doggedly marched on until struck down."

When the first column was pillaged, another advanced.

"Although everyone knew," Miller wrote, "that within a few minutes he would be beaten down, perhaps killed, I could detect no sign of wavering or fear. They marched steadily, with heads up, without the encouragement of music or cheering or any possibility that they might escape serious injury or death. The police rushed out and methodically and mechanically beat down the second column. There was no fight, no struggle; the marchers simply walked forward till struck down."[37]

This somewhat gruesome image can also stand as a measure of the incredible power of a belief system. There is no shortage of models available if we only look.

Arthur Ashe, a model in his own right, greatly admired an outstanding example of a man who "walked his talk", Nelson Mandela. Ashe, in his book, *Days of Grace*, writes of Mandela:

"To have spent twenty-seven years in jail for political reasons, to have been deprived of the whole mighty center of one's life, and then to emerge apparently without a trace of bitterness, alert and ready to lead

one's country forward, may be the most extraordinary individual human achievement that I have witnessed in my lifetime. I marvel that he could come out of jail free of bitterness and yet uncompromising in his basic political beliefs; I marvel at this ability to combine an impeccable character, to which virtually everyone attests, with the political wisdom of a Solomon. In jail, I am told, his white guards came to have such respect for him that in some ways he was their warden and they the prisoners, more prisoners of apartheid." [38]

If we are to look to the essence, the heart, the soul of an individual, we must examine his belief system. The belief system tells us his personality, his habits, but most of all, his character. It is to the person's character that we look if we allow ourselves to engage in one of the highest forms of human interaction—trust. At any level of relationship—family, friendship, business or spiritual—it is trust that stands at the center of the union. Without trust, the relationship deteriorates. With trust, aided by attention, the relationship develops. With trust, individuals can engage in new behaviors and even modify their own beliefs.

Mahatma Gandhi again stands as the shining model of this thesis. When his countrymen were in great turmoil, with the conflict between the Muslims and the Hindus at their greatest intensity, with Indians maiming and slaughtering one another, this simple man went day after day into villages to preach tolerance and understanding. At extraordinary risk to himself, Gandhi practiced what he believed. Millions of Indians could not fail to see, understand, believe, trust. It should be understood, that Gandhi's message was not propagated by radio or television. There was no massive advertising campaign promoting his concepts—no Madison Avenue promotion or spin put on his message. Just a man in

a loin cloth, willing to be jailed for his beliefs, willing to go on
life-threatening hunger strikes, willing to walk across the
country, all for the sake of what he believed. Hundred's of
millions of Indians, who could neither read nor write,
perceived his devotion to their cause as a reason to pay
attention. Millions of Indians came to trust him, tens of
thousands were willing to give up their lives for him. They
believed in the man and his character. Such is the power of
beliefs.

CHANGING BELIEF SYSTEMS

Create doubt

When any of us encounter information that contradicts
our beliefs, we have two choices. We can become defensive
and exclude data that implies that we may have been incor-
rect. This action limits our ability to change, adapt and develop. On the other hand, we can examine the contradictory
information to determine whether it might be true. Allowing new data to enter our 'script' can be incredibly valuable.
Let's take the example of a chronic pain patient who intensely believes that she will become worse if she moves.
Until her admission to a rehabilitation setting, she had been
sitting, reclining or lying down, virtually all the time. This
inactivity and the concurrent belief that movement will only
aggravate her condition, is reinforced by pain experienced
with any movement. In the context of a secure rehabilitation
setting, she was able to increase her range of motion and
strength and to decrease her muscle tightness. In this situation some patients tenaciously cling to their fear and belief,
stating that these improvements have not really eliminated
the pain and are therefore meaningless. Others, acknowledge the new information and consider the new percep-

tion—a belief that in spite of continued pain, it may be possible to increase overall activity and therefore quality of life.

THE RESISTANCE OF BELIEFS TO CHANGE

Beliefs can be incredibly stubborn. There is a story told by Abraham Maslow that illustrates the point clearly. According to Maslow, a psychiatrist was treating a patient who believed that he was a corpse. In spite of the psychiatrist's best logic and effort, the patient continued with his bizarre perception. Finally in desperation the psychiatrist asked the patient, "Do corpse bleed?" "That's absurd," replied the patient, "Corpses do not bleed." After getting the patients permission the psychiatrist proceeded to prick the man's finger with a pin producing a drop of blood. Staring at the blood for a moment, the patient turned to the psychiatrist and exclaimed, "I'll be damned, corpses do bleed."

Another example of our selective absorption of information was illustrated in a commentary on the National Public Radio program *Morning Edition.* The commentator was describing his suburban neighbor's ritual of locking four locks on his front door each morning to secure the safety and security of the family home. The neighbor then proceeded to drive away without using his safety belt. The same neighbor, the journalist noted, also checked each bottle of over-the-counter medication carefully to determine whether it had been tampered with arsenic. His cautiousness, however, did not extend to his purchase of poultry which, by statistical probability, has a hundred times more chance of causing serious harm. The man's belief that danger from criminals was very real had been much reinforced by the media while other information such as the danger of eating tainted poultry had not been absorbed. The commentator reported that his neighbor continued to behave in a manner that he could not help but believe was illogical.

Beliefs are especially difficult to change when they are tied to a cue and the cue is recurrent. Take the common belief that pain is physical. Pain is typically associated with an injury or a physical diagnosis. Our senses tell us that, a moment before the injury, no pain existed and now, following the physical injury, pain is present. Our previous experiences with pain have also reinforced this simple and seemingly logical interpretation. This is the picture that I confront when I discuss pain with chronic pain patients. None have had previous training in the analysis of pain (as is actually quite true of most physicians). None have ever heard a discussion that in any way contradicts their beliefs concerning pain. If rehabilitation staffs are to have any chance of long-term rehabilitation, they must facilitate a change in the patient's beliefs. Generally, patients believe that medication and medical science provide the only hope for improvement and, without such successful intervention, they are doomed to a lifetime of pain. Implicit in this interpretation is the belief that pain is physical and therefore *outside of the realm of their control.* In order for health professionals to acquire any possibility of increased activity, pain and stress management or rehabilitation in general, they must work to change the patient's beliefs regarding pain. They must help him establish a new belief system and to understand that pain management *is within the realm of his control.*

The dynamics of creating a change in the patient's belief system are to create doubt in their own system. Early in the treatment of each chronic pain patient I tell the following story:

> One of the most vivid illustrations of the complexity of pain is the practice of *couvade.* *Couvade,* observed by anthropologist in cultures

across the world, is the event of women bearing children with virtually no sign of distress. In an extreme example, a woman may toil in the fields until the newborn's head begins to crown. Returning to her home, the mother informs the father that the baby is about to be born. At which point the husband gets into bed and moans and groans as though he were in great pain while the mother bears the child. In some cases, the father remains in bed following the birth to recover from his terrible ordeal while the mother immediately returns to the field to attend the crops.[39]

Such an incredible example raises difficult questions for those who profess that pain is simply a neurological impulse resulting from injury to body tissue. Is it really true that the woman experiences no pain in spite of the fact that she is undergoing a physical ordeal? Is it true that the husband experiences real pain? For those who argue that the women indeed must have pain but the man, who has no physiological experience of birth, does not have pain, let me ask whether morning sickness commonly reported by *husbands* in our culture is real? I have no doubt that the husbands of pregnant women experiencing nausea and vomiting would affirm the reality of their experience.

When lecturing to medical students and medical residents, I often extend the dilemma by asking whether a hysterically blind patient is truly blind and, if one does not believe in the veracity of the blindness, would you sent this "blind" person across a busy street? I have never heard anyone respond affirmatively to this question. If we can observe the tangible evidence of sympathetic morning sickness and accept the reality of a hysterical blindness, than why not the integrity of the man's pain in the *couvade* practicing culture? Why not accept the women's lack of pain?

Another story almost universally told within chronic pain programs takes place on Anzio Beach during World War II. This setting was the location of horrific American losses. Lieutenant Colonel Henry Beecher observed that there was an extraordinary inconsistency between the seriousness of wounds and the intensity of the solder's pain. Present during the horrors of battle, Lieutenant Colonel Beecher, later Professor at the Harvard School of Medicine, found that among seriously wounded soldiers who were questioned within twelve hours of battle wound, 25 percent reported only slight pain and 32 percent no pain at all. He found that over half of the seriously wounded soldiers requested no medication.

In 1946, Dr. Beecher published his observations in a classic article entitled *"The Pain in Men Wounded in Battle"*[40] which was to change our understanding of pain. He stated that one hypothesis, that the men were in shock, was clearly unlikely as the symptoms of shock are easily discernable. To make matters more puzzling, Dr. Beecher has written that upon his return to a private practice of medicine in New Jersey, he often encountered patients with very small injuries (finger cuts, for example) who requested large quantities of analgesics. The contrast is that of soldiers experiencing major wounds requesting no pain-killers and civilians with small wounds requesting large amounts of narcotic medication.

I continue telling stories progressing to stories more similar to the everyday experiences of the patients. In doing so, I am attempting to cast doubt on chronic pain as a purely physical experience. The belief that pain is purely physical limits the ability to gain control of pain. The belief that pain

is purely physical is not supported by our scientific understanding.

You may have started with a belief that pain is physical. If
you were my patient I would try to persuade you that pain is
actually a combination of physical, emotional and cognitive
factors—a perception that allows for more leverage in the
management of pain. The belief that pain is more complex
than simply neurological input is difficult for many people
to accept but, once accepted, it permits new options—something that often happens with new beliefs. If I have been
successful in creating doubt in your original belief, you may
be more subject to accept David Morris' statement, *"By taking
back responsibility for how we understand pain, we can recover the
power to relieve it. "[41]* People don't change people. Ideas change
people.

You may remember the case study of Robert K. who believed his spine would shatter if he moved too fast. He believed his doctor had told him that would happen. After
three weeks of intensive treatment, Robert left rehabilitation walking over ten miles a day as measured by a pedom-
eter placed on his ankle. His range of motion was significantly improved and he proudly showed any willing observer
that he could move his head substantially in all directions.
His depression was gone and he was detoxified from all of
his medication. How did such changes occur? Robert had
what I call a "belief-ectomy"—that is a removal of his previous
strongly entrenched belief.

This perceptual change was of the most importance, if
not *the* most critical change that occurred in Robert's rehabilitation. His original belief originated while he was very
vulnerable (frightened and anxious) and came from an authority figure (his physician). Now, in the presence of other
authority figures (in the rehabilitation setting), Robert systematically received information contradictory to his origi-

nal beliefs ("It is safe and beneficial for you to move in spite of the discomfort"). Specifically the information was, "You moved one centimeter in this direction yesterday. You can safely move two centimeters today. We have thoroughly examined you. Two centimeters today will not damage you, although it might hurt." The need to proceed slowly was crucial both for safely and belief reasons. Robert experienced pain when he moved his neck and pain to him meant injury. It had always meant that damage was being done to the body and should be avoided. In Robert's chronic condition, however, avoidance of movement only contributed to his already extremely tight and painful condition. In order to rehabilitate Robert, we had to systematically change his belief. Two factors were necessary. Robert had to be provided with new information and he had to be willing to receive it.

Remember Amy S. Amy was the patient who had a diagnosis of Ankylosing Spondylosis early in her life and believed that she was condemned to a life of pain, embarrassment and disability. She believed that her physician told her that her condition was irreversible and would only worsen with age. Her mental state deteriorated and her physical status came to meet her feared expectations. Without the coordinated efforts of a rehabilitation team it is unlikely that Amy would have improved. At the beginning of therapy she was fearful but persisted because of the support of the therapeutic team. The structure and security of the program were critical in allowing Amy to test her limits and to make gains. Before and after video-taped recordings of Amy's posture and movement were incredible in their contrast.

In three weeks of intense treatment, Amy reduced her pain behaviors (rubbing her back, facial grimaces of pain and reddening of her face), improved her body mechanics, established a new home activity schedule and increased upper body strength and range of motion. Most importantly, she established a new belief regarding her diagnosis. While

continuing to understand that some Ankylosing Spondylosis existed, the majority of her dysfunction was from myofascial
pain patterns and therefore was highly reversible. Amy left
rehabilitation with only a slight forward bent, able to look
others straight in the eye. Two years later, while steadfastly
maintaining a daily exercise regimen, Amy continued to be
free of narcotics and alcohol and was walking upright.

Changing Robert and Amy 's belief system was critical.
In many ways changing their beliefs were more important
than changing their behavior for their behaviors were based
upon their beliefs. Without a change in their beliefs, any
changes in their behavior would likely be temporary.

Examining how beliefs were so critical to the lives of
Robert and Amy can teach us an important lesson. We too
need to examine our beliefs and to be open to alternative
and perhaps contrary information

Like Robert and Amy we are often unaware of the beliefs that
govern our lives. We experience the trials and pleasures of
life, giving little thought to how we process these experiences. By identifying and examining our beliefs we can discover the driving force behind our behavior.

Uncovering one's beliefs is difficult. One way to identify
them is to answer questions such as the following:

1. How would you assess your life? Has it been worthwhile?
   What would other people whom you feel are important
   say regarding the importance of your life?
2. Do you feel that you are a good human being? If yes, what
   makes you believe so? Can you write down actions that
   ·support your belief?
3. Have you had circumstances that held you back? Were the
   circumstances under your control?

4. What are the obstacles that prevent you from reaching the goals you have set for your life? Are the obstacles external or internal?

5. Regardless of your achievements, do you hold a set of values that you believe are worthwhile?

Taking the time to answer the above question can provide a window to your beliefs. Remember, beliefs can be as simple as "I'm a worthwhile person" or "I'm a "failure." If your set of beliefs is negative and not constructive to your well-being, it may be time to seriously examine whether your perceptions are absolutely correct. Maybe those around you see you as a person of worth, while you only see your shortcomings. It may be time to be open to new information.

I commit myself to take care of myself for the sake of myself, my family, my friends, my community and my country.

Chapter 6

MODELS: LEARNING FROM OTHERS'

BLUEPRINTS

IN April of 1997 a controversy arose regarding the creation
of a new statue celebrating Franklin Delano Roosevelt. The
debate centered on the sculptor's depiction of Roosevelt
without the leg braces he had worn since age 37. During
Roosevelt's 12 years as President, many Americans were strik-
ingly unaware of the extent of Roosevelt's disability. In her
book *No Ordinary Times* biographer Doris Kearns Goodwin
describes an experience not atypical of the time:

> *"The actor Gregory Peck recalled waiting at a habor*
> *when he was a boy to catch his first glimpse of the*
> *President. Like most Americans, Peck had no idea that*
> *Roosevelt was a paraplegic. While he knew that*
> *Roosevelt had polio when he was younger, he had no*
> *understanding of the full extent of his disability, no*

idea that he had to call for his valet every morning to
help him get out of bed. Because there was an unspo-
ken code of honor on the part of the press never to
photograph the President looking crippled, never to
show him helpless, never to show him on his crutches
or in his wheelchair, most people simply assumed that
the polio had left him a bit lame but that he could still
walk on his own power." [42]

Over fifty years later we can admire the extraordinary courage of the President, the respect and genuine warmth provided by the press. We can understand that their behavior
represented the custom of the time. We can also quickly
conclude that such cooperation and deception could not
occur in modern politics.

As the controversy over his statue indicates, some Americans still wish to remember Franklin Delano Roosevelt as a
leader untarnished by any weakness. Other Americans, such
as a spokesman for the country's disabled people protested,
citing the symbolic importance of the braces in the hearts of
Americans who have disabilities.

What difference does this make? Why the argument over
one more statue of a widely acclaimed politician?—because
symbols and models are important to our identity, to our
character and ultimately to our behaviors. Those images
which convey values that we admire provide meaning to our
lives. For people who have disabilities, it is important to have
public symbols which state that a man in a wheelchair could
become President of the United States. It is important to
know that courage and perseverance can overcome adversity.

The point becomes more obvious when we examine how
models can affect specific people. Historian Goodman writes
of a trip Franklin Roosevelt made to visit the American troops
late in World War II when he was in ill health himself:

*"Roosevelt generally allowed himself to be seen in pub-
lic in only two situations—either standing with his
braces locked, or seated in an open car. But here, in the
presence of so many young amputees, he was willing
to reveal his vulnerability, to let them see that he was as
crippled as they. 'With a cheering smile to each of them,'
Sam Rosenman, the President's aide observed, 'and a
pleasant word at the bedside of a score or more, this
man who had risen from a bed of helplessness ultimately to become President of the United States and
leader of the free world was living proof of what the
human spirit could do'."[43]*

Sam Rosenman, the President's aide, claimed he had never
seen the President with tears in his eyes, but that afternoon
"he was close to them." Undoubtedly, the young men were
similarly moved.

The challenges that FDR faced a half a century ago are
perhaps more evident to most American's through their
knowledge of Christopher Reeve. On Memorial Day, 1995,
the news services flashed the dramatic story that Reeve,
known to virtually every American for his film portrayal of
Superman, had been thrown from his horse during a riding
competition. For days, the public waited to hear of his survival and then the extent of his paralysis. Undoubtedly, this
strapping six foot four actor had become so identified with
his signature character that we watched not only the vulnerability of the actor but were confused with his image as well.
"The Man of Steel", as every school child knows, can leap tall
buildings in a single bound and certainly can tolerate a fall
from a horse. But Christopher Reeve is not Superman. He is
an actor, a man, a human being. And human beings cannot
tolerate a "C1-C2"—a designation referring to the paralyzing
injury between the first and second cervical vertebrae and

sometimes known as the "hangman's injury." Reeve himself states, *"It was as if I'd been hanged, cut down and sent to rehab."*[44]

Like Roosevelt, Reeve was extremely physical prior to his injury. Flying, sailing, scuba diving and horseback riding in addition to a full schedule of working for such causes as the environment, children's issues, human rights and the National Endowment for the Arts were activities tacked onto his highly successful acting career. He too had to rise from the ashes of depression—from those early hours when he thought,

> *"This can't be my life. There's been a mistake."* Reeve said, *"When they told me what my condition was, I felt that I was no longer a human being. Then Dana (his wife) came into my room and knelt down to the level of my bed. We made eye contact. I said, 'Maybe this isn't worth it. Maybe I should just check out.' And she was crying and she said, 'But you're still you, and I love you.' And that saved my life."*

Defining moments are good for movies. In real life these benchmarks are followed by struggle. A day in Reeve's life provides a small measure of his battle. He begins each and every day strapped to a six-foot board followed by many hours of arduous physical and pulmonary exercise. The most basic of bodily functions are performed by others that require, for Reeve, not only physical but psychological strength of Herculean proportions. His nights offer little reduction in his struggle:

> *"Usually I don't fall asleep till well after midnight. I have to be turned every three or four hours during the night to prevent the skin from breaking down. If the nurses are gentle enough, I won't wake up. I have to sleep at a 90° angle on my side. If I were lying on my*

back, the weight of my body could create another decu-
bitus wound, and I don't want to go through that
again. . . . Sometimes I'll spasm while they turn me.
The effect of a spasm, the tension of it, goes straight to
my neck. It stiffens like a tree trunk. If I'm awake, I'll
ask the nurse to give me a soft-tissue massage, which
goes deep into the muscles. I have to take about 12
kinds of pills plus Metamucil. Pills to help control the
spasms. Pills to prevent infection in the stool. And so
on. [45]

When one reads of the physical and emotional ordeal of
Christopher Reeve, one's own personal issues can be put
into a different perspective. Life's gifts can be treasured and
the depth of character of the Christoper Reeves of the world
can be truly admired. Personally, my mind is struck by his
psychological adaptation and adjustment to his incredible
burden. He has chosen an optimistic approach, an appreciation for what he has, a victimless role, great perspective and
meaningful goals. He has chosen to actively participate in
life with its limitations and to serve others in the ways that he
is capable.

I doubt if Christopher Reeve thinks of himself as a model
any more than did Eleanor Roosevelt, Susan B. Anthony,
Mahatma Gandhi, Mother Teresa, or Martin Luther King.
Theirs was a more focused mission. But individuals with high
visibility often have the label "model" placed on them
whether it is their intention or not. Modeling is a process.
Whether the model is Martin Luther King or Dennis Rod-
man, someone will learn something from each model.

Many college students exposed to Introductory Psychology will recall the research on modeling conducted by Albert
Bandura. Bandura's careful investigations provided landmark
evidence of the power of modeling in the learning process.
Young children, typically ages 3 to 6, were exposed to a model

aggressively striking a large inflated doll with a mallet. The degree to which they acquired and performed this behavior was measured. By manipulating variables such as the types of models (adults, cartoons, etc.) and the consequence following the modeled behavior (reward or punishment), Bandura was able to dramatically show that, given the proper circumstances, children not only immediately learned the aggressive acts but, under certain conditions, exhibited their retention six months later.

In one classic study, boys tended to show a greater incidence of aggression immediately following the viewing of the model. However, when provided an incentive (a reward), the girls showed that they had indeed "learned" as much as the boys. In other words, both boys and girls had apparently acquired the same information. Boys were more prone to perform the aggression they had learned. Girls, on the other hand, initially inhibited their aggression but, when provided an incentive, demonstrated that they had been equally influenced by the model. It seems that, even when not initially apparent, learning occurred.[46]

The power of models is immense, often subtle, sometimes totally unconscious and always a tremendous influence on society. Of course, like all power, it can be used constructively or destructively. For every Gandhi there is a Hitler, for every Mother Teresa there is an Idi Amin.

The influence of most models is probably covert, subtle and, when negative, pernicious. The characteristics exemplified by the Franklin Delano Roosevelts and Christopher Reeves of the world, as presented here, are very positive and easily labeled—courage, determination, strength, perseverance. Not all models are so positive.

Clinical psychologist Mary Pipher, in her revealing portrayal of the American adolescent girl in her best-selling book *Reviving Ophelia,* persuasively states that today's young women differ little from their predecessors in the rules taught to them: *"Be attractive, be a lady, be unselfish and of service, make relationships work and be competent without complaint."* This message is what psychotherapist Terrence Real calls the *"suppression of the voice."* During a time when some argue that the opportunities for women are far beyond what previous generations could imagine, how could such reactionary beliefs continue in such strength? On the one hand our young women are told that they are equal and yet a different message is learned—the message that their worth is based upon appearance, subservience, and inhibition of their opinion. How does this occur?

The answer is straightforward and clear. Pipher states:

> *"They model themselves after media stars, not parental ideals. With puberty, girls face enormous cultural pressure to split into false selves. The pressure comes from schools, magazines, music, television, advertisements and movies . . . In public they become who they are supposed to be."*[47]

Describing a typical adolescent girl frequenting her office for therapy, Pipher cites the endless influence of videos focused on the breasts, derrieres, and cleavage of multiple young women hanging adoringly over rock stars, music which features explicit subservient female sexual roles, and an exhausting diet of mindless television fare depicting women's primary role as seducing men into either sex or marriage. One does not have to be conservative to realize that such constant fare can be assimilated into the minds of America's youth.

Not all young women are contaminated by the influences of the media. Read what psychologist Pipher writes of a young women who appeared to protect herself from the cultural pressure:

"Lori was independent and funny. She made con-
scious choices about sex, drugs and alcohol. In fact,
she made conscious choices about everything. She looked
within herself for guidance and answers. Lori already
had sorted her experiences into what she could and
couldn't control, and she knew how to screen out what
was beyond her control. She had a sense of who she
was and an orientation toward her future." [48]

In the potentially destructive adolescent world described by Pipher, the distinction between constructive and destructive behaviors is clear. While other factors play a significant role in the complicated process of growing up, the role of models is critical. Those young women described by Pipher as living chaotic, sad, and insecure lives were much more likely to have come under the menacing influence of negative models in our culture. The young women who weather and even grow during this potential stormy period of life, proactively and overtly choose positive models. Just as significant is the fact that they also restrict their exposure to the corrosive influence of the negative models.

As adults we can mistakenly believe that our cognitive abilities protect us from those messages that we do not condone. The statistics of our society do not support such a conclusion. "Lookism" (the view that we are more worthwhile if we look like media depicted beautiful people), prejudice in race and gender and desensitization to violence are nurtured by routine exposure. It is up to each of us as individuals to realize the harmful effect of the media and take personal decisive action in controlling it in our own lives.

It is not enough to attend to the positive models available to every one of us. Like second hand smoke, we must recognize the harm inflicted by pervasive negative models. We must take charge of the information and values we allow to affect us. Messages of violence, sexism, intolerance, exploitation, greed and materialism are no less damaging than physical poisons entering our body.

I do not propose an external censorship, but an internal one. Taking charge of your life means making conscious choices about what you allow to influence your mind, your body and your soul. Proactively choosing your models and censoring those potential negative models is your decision.

Television is perhaps the most villainous example. In a world permeated by mindless sitcoms and action dramas heavily laced with violence and sexual innuendoes, local news programs monopolized by murder, mayhem and molestation, and a paucity of consistent positive models, this media is the most destructive. We are told by social scientists that we spend eight to nine hours each day working and commuting, eight hours or so sleeping and two hours eating. The remaining five to six hours has been increasingly absorbed by television. The same social scientists inform us that children and adolescents have less contact with adults than even a generation ago and that, "During the past 25 years, adolescents have lost 16 hours of parental time each week." It appears the need for positive models has never been greater.

Television and the media are common whipping boys for the ills of our society. However, the commonness of the criticism does not change the truth that the models coming from our media are largely responsible for the increase in violence and sexism in our society. Its influence on our mores, its ability to mold public information and its impact on the minds of our children has been extensively documented by our social scientists. Nevertheless, we appear powerless to control its influence. It's as if all of the good that stems from the first amendment of our constitution has turned around and bitten us—as if the nation has become addicted (as it undoubtedly has).

Fifty years ago, few Americans were persuaded that smoking had much of a deleterious effect. Even when the evidence began to emerge that smoking was a direct cause for multiple diseases, we continued to rationalize our behavior. Social gatherings were thick with smoke and there was little concern about its effect. The public scoffed at attempts to alter smoking habits. We look back now and realize that we had allowed ourselves to be duped by insidious and even duplicitous information. Yet tremendous strides have been made in reversing our nation's consumption of this poison. If such an extraordinary pattern as smoking can be altered, then surely the same can be accomplished with our habits concerning the media.

If you wish to take charge of your life, it is important to choose positive models on the one hand and personally censor negative models and images on the other. Each commitment requires some follow through.

CHOOSING POSITIVE MODELS

Choosing a positive model can be easy. Benefiting from that model in our daily lives can be another thing altogether. The first step in establishing the benefits of a model is to become very knowledgeable about the life and times of your model. Write out your model's characteristics, virtues and, very importantly, his failings. Know the struggles and obstacles he overcame. Gain a comprehensive understanding of his life.

People who know me well are aware of my extraordinary admiration for Mahatma Gandhi. I have read numerous biographies, viewed documentaries and watched the film depicting his life many, many times. This knowledge affords me a wealth of guidelines in a variety of settings. I know of Gandhi's physical struggles, the gradual evolution of his

philosophy, his patience in his country's battles, his tolerance of others of differing views, his ability to adjust, his vora-
cious reading, his determination and many other qualities.
He was not perfect but his failings were few.

In order to benefit from the teachings and examples of
a model, one must have an intimate knowledge of the model's
life. Models can be used constructively by allowing them to
serve as guides, inspiration and perspective. The question,
"What would Gandhi do in this situation?" may seem silly to
others but not to me. My knowledge of his life does not give
me a specific behavior to follow but a tone. It reminds me of
characteristics like perseverance, determination, honesty to
one's vision, etc. With these thoughts in mind, my decisions
are easier. My awareness that Gandhi was a man whose philosophy evolved over many decades, that his goals were im-
perfectly met and that he lived through periods of sadness,
allows me to put many of my own problems in perspective.
His humanness and determination inspire me.

Gandhi followed some practices that are inappropriate
to my life. His view of technology now appears simplistic in
our more complicated age. His personal habits of celibacy
and a daily salt enema for over forty years were peculiar to his
time, needs, and culture. Nevertheless, I can learn, be guided
and take strength from this incredible human being.

Choosing a model for yourself depends on your own life
and goals. What path do you wish to follow in your life? What
are the characteristics that you most value? What models can
you learn about in great depth?

I have depicted models we all know—Mahatma Gandhi,
Helen Keller, Harry Truman and Eleanor Roosevelt, among
others. Models chosen from our relatives, friends, or work,
can be in many ways be more valuable, for you experience
them in the flesh and blood. The critical feature is to learn as
much as you can about their lives and allow that knowledge

to be one additional way in which you take charge of your own life.

As you explore your personal repertoire of men and women you admire, be alert to your body. Those models whose images inspire even the slightest general physical comfort, warmth in the chest or a state of well-being, should be given special attention. Your body has its own knowledge and can be a special cue to those models whose impact on you can be the greatest for you.

RESTRICTING NEGATIVE MODELS

The second half of using models effectively in your life is to protect yourself from those messages and images of models inconsistent with your values. Critics might argue that such an effort is unrealistic for we are bombarded with information. These critics underestimate both the importance of the task and the nature of the goal. Restricting negative information is not hiding your head in the sand. It is an effort to make contact with a real world—the world of meaningful feelings, relationships and values.

The areas in which the media distorts our reality are many. One of the most profound is the increase in distrust, fear and paranoia promulgated by television. This is described in a recent book by Gaven De Becker, *The Gift of Fear*, which documents the huge discrepancy between the public's fears and the statistical probability of real calamity. He indicts the media for the creation of much of our hysteria:

> *"Television in most major cities devotes up to 40 hours a day to telling us about those who have fallen prey to some disaster and to exploring what calamities may be coming next. The local news anchor should begin each evening's broadcast by saying, 'Welcome to the*

news; we're surprised you made it through another day. Here's what happened to those who didn't.' Each day we learn what the new studies reveal: 'Cellular phones can kill you'; 'The dangers of debit card'; 'Contaminated Thanksgiving turkey kills family of three. Could your family be next?'" [49]

The world created by the media is an unreal world, a world in which physical beauty, artificial relationships, sexual gratification, and materialism are elevated to a position of need while long-term relationships, spiritual values, character and sustained effort are relegated to the status of "boring." It is unfortunate for our society that so many of us have been persuaded by this illusion.

The extreme levels that television has gone to attract viewers would be funny if it wasn't actually sad. Many years ago I asked a friend of my teenage daughter to join us on a trip to Europe. At the time, one or two European cities had been hit by random violence. The young woman's mother, obviously influenced by the frequent and dramatic media reports of the violence, refused to allow her daughter to go. She would, however, allow her daughter to accompany us to New York City, a place in which the likelihood of violence was more than 20 times that of any city we would have visited in Europe. Psychiatrist Robert Coles has written that children in some parts of the United States are more frightened than children in Lebanon or Northern Ireland. [50]

I have chosen to focus on television because of its ubiquitous nature. The fact that the average American watches between 25 and 30 hours each week is astounding. Its dominance in airports, hotel lobbies, sporting events and the living room of the American home makes it worthy of the attention I have given it. But other media also impact our consciousness and ultimately influence who we are.

Negative models impart covert messages that may not be immediately recognized but over time have a tremendous impact. Author and psychologist Mary Pipher writes of the messages conveyed by the movie *Medicine Man*, a story of a male scientist who is in the rain forest searching for a cure for cancer:

> *"Sean Connery is visited by a female scientist forty years younger then he, wearing short shorts and a tight, low-cut top. He's shocked to find that a scientist is female and refuses to work with her. She's snooty and terrified of snakes. Then she has an accident, Sean saves her, and she falls weeping into his arms. Reduced to a helpless blob of jelly, the female scientist becomes more feminine and likable. She follows Sean around and he rewards her with smiles and caresses. In the end she gives up her career to help him find the cure for cancer."*[51]

This movie does not stand up and shout that women are inferior—that they are sex objects whose primary role is to serve and support the intellectually superior man or that his career is more important then hers. It does not overtly state that her sense of worthiness is based upon the acceptance of a man. But it most certainly does convey these messages. Undoubtedly, much of the audience just enjoyed this movie at a superficial level. However, the messages expressed by this and the enormous number of similar media have their effect. The cultural stereotype presented by the media has a reality but it is not my reality and I choose not to expose myself to it any more than is absolutely necessary. In this fashion I take another step in controlling my mind and my life.

The very act of reducing contact with the media provides additional benefits as well—time to engage in listening, talking and interacting with others. It offers the opportunity to actively engage in life as opposed to passively watching others. Most importantly, it takes back control. We often hear people praise the valuable characteristics of television only to lament how much time it takes from their lives. How seductive those moments of pleasure are in controlling significant portions of our wakening hours. I can only wonder how many of us, if asked in the 1940's before the advent of television, if we would willingly give up 25 to 30 hours of our time to this medium each week, would answer "yes." And yet we have gradually done just that.

At the end of each chapter of this book is the pledge "I commit myself to take care of myself for the sake of myself, my family, my friends, my community and my nation." I cannot think of a more poignant test for you to begin the process of taking care of yourself and influencing those around you (especially if you have children) than to drastically reduce your exposure to television.

CHOOSING POSITIVE MODELS

Take a moment to consider what people you truly admire. Promise yourself that you will take the time to learn more about their lives, paying special attention to their character, principles, values and failings. As a start on this goal, complete the forms on the following pages.

Choosing Positive Models

Someone I Greatly Admire:

_____

Characteristics that I admire in the person I have chosen:

_____

Obstacles my model has overcome:

_____

Imperfections or failing in his/her life:

_____

Limiting Negative Models

Step 1: Measure the number of hours you watch television during a one-week period.

Mon	Tue	Wed	Thurs	Fri	Sat	Sun

Total _____ per week.

Step 2: If you consider the total hours of television viewing to be excessive following your measure of one week, begin to regularly monitor your use of television in an effort to reduce its impact.

Step 3: Write down the programs that you typically watch which provide positive models.

Step 4: Write down the programs that you typically watch which provide negative models.

Step 5: Write down any negative models that you have observed during the past week in media other than television.

I commit myself to take care of myself for the sake of myself, my family, my friends, my community and my country.

Chapter 7

WHO ARE YOU?

IN Stanley Kubick's film *2001:A Space Oddessy* the major an-
tagonist is HAL, an extraordinary computer that can guide a
space ship to distant galaxies as well as control the environment of its inhabitants. As the film progresses, HAL "de-
cides" that his mission takes precedent over that of the crew
and that some of them are dispensable. HAL's ability to converse, to calculate and to make decisions is wondrously intelligent, but there remains a problem—he lacks moral sense.
He lacks character.

In the television series *Star Trek* a further evolution of
the computer takes the form of an android named Data. Data
is a marvel of sophistication but lacks certain human elements such as the ability to understand humor and to be silly.
For all of his ability to analyze information beyond any single
human's comprehension, Data is unable is to be more human—to feel, to love and to be sensitive.

We are different—different from machines and different from each other. Each of us is a unique bundle of molecules arranged in individual packages, with our own history and special spirit. Unfortunately, many of us spend a lifetime more concerned about our differences and worrying about how we can be more similar. We spend time fretting over our failings and ignoring our strengths.

Have you ever watched a sunset, immersed in the beauty of the experience? Have you felt awe in the presence of the Grand Canyon or the autumn of New England? These are magnificent experiences, inspiring wonder at nature's ability to bring together so many elements with symmetry and grandeur. During each such experience we allow ourselves to focus on many dimensions—color, texture, light variations, vastness, harmony, power, subtlety, proportion. We look, sense and feel the presence of each setting believing that it is truly unique and, of course, we are right.

If we contemplate our motives in seeking out nature, we may speculate that we have a desire to see the unusual, to experience the unfamiliar or to escape from the pressures and stresses of our daily lives. Each feeling for nature, however, is already in us and is brought forth by our focus on the experience at hand. At that moment we appreciate the uniqueness of what we are attending. This heightened sensitivity is available to us at other times if we choose to avail ourselves of its benefit.

It is interesting to note that what we take for granted might be considered beautiful and even astonishing by others unfamiliar with our environment. Imagine the wonder that an aborigine would have when seeing our homes, our work or our electronics. Imagine what an 18th-century American would experience if he or she were to see a soda can, a vending machine, an automobile or an airplane. Each would focus so intently on the nuances and the many dimensions of his study that for the moment, all other sensations would be blocked out. They would probably feel wonder and amazement. Since each would bring his own unique history, each would create his own experience.

The great men and women so often mentioned in this book are unique—each is a composite of heredity and environment never duplicated. The same can be said for any of us. Like each setting in nature, there is only one of us with our combination of our genes, environment and experience. Each grain of sand in the desert is different from all others and, if we look closely enough, we too are unique. We must attend and focus to appreciate this uniqueness and we must learn to set aside the familiar.

Familiarity allows us to function and to adapt. However, in the process we lose our sensitivity. It is of great value for us to reacquaint ourselves with the complexity, nuances, and uniqueness of our being. To see with new sight takes effort and practice. It means serious introspection, writing out of thoughts and talking with those we trust.

Here are two exercises to facilitate this process. The first I encountered as a young psychologist as a means of helping others get in touch with basic values. More recently it has been popularized in the writings of author Stephen Covey. The idea is to write your own eulogy. Ideally, you'll find the process more inspirational than somber. Divide a piece of paper into three columns, with the third column widest, and label them "role", "name" and "eulogy."

In the first column list the various major roles that you play in your life, such as mother, father, daughter, son, employee, employer/supervisor, friend, citizen, church member—whatever roles you find significant. In the second column, choose someone who knows your actions in that role— your children, parents, relatives, friends, co-workers, etc. Now the hard part. I want you to put down this book and really get into this. Take at least 10 minutes (set a timer) and write out what you *would like* each significant person in your life to say at your funeral. Notice I did not ask that you write out what they *would* say at this time, but what you *would like* them to say.

When you complete writing what you would like others to say about you at your funeral, allow yourself to mentally examine the qualities that you value. Do you want others to remember your warmth, caring, fortitude, determination, integrity, loyalty, good humor, fairness, honesty, empathy, generosity, strength, reliability, trust, charm, guts, courage, or perseverance? Be generous with yourself. One action can represent one of your personal qualities. Don't worry, no one need see your list unless you choose to show it. Keep it handy. We'll be returning to it shortly.

Many years ago, I was employed as the Associate Director of West Virginia University Medical Center Pain Clinic. In that setting we evaluated and treated a large number of low back pain patients who worked in the mines of West Virginia. One man who stands out in my mind was the West Virginia state-sheep-shearing champion who had held the title for many years running. This man in his late 30's was stooped over and complained of low back pain. He did not, however, wish any intervention that would in any way interrupt his sheep shearing. That was his passion in life. Although it was obvious even to him that the hours of bending over in a contorted fashion were the cause of his constant aches, it was not enough for him to stop. Each year, almost like clockwork, he would come to the pain clinic to see if we had any new innovations that might provide some relief from his unrelenting pain. Never did he consider the possibility of stopping the cause of his back pain.

The sheep-shearing champion was not truly a chronic pain sufferer as defined by pain clinics across the United States. While it is true he had pain and it was chronic, he had none of the other characteristics so common of the chronic pain population. He was not inactive, depressed, dependent on medication, going from doctor to doctor, having difficulty with his sleep—virtually none of the co-existing symptoms we observe with chronic pain patients who are overwhelmed by their pain. How could that be? After all, he had back pain every day of his life.

The answer may be obvious to you—he had passion, direction and purpose. He was the state champion and would show you his shearing technique at the drop of a hat, tell you how many sheep he could clip in a hour and gladly provide any other detail that you wished to hear. His life was sheep shearing first and pain second or maybe fifth. He didn't have time to allow the pain to dominate.

I don't tell this story to my patients because I believe they would be offended by it. They would tell me that everyone has a different tolerance for pain or that the sheep shearer's pain was not as severe as theirs or that I'm trying to imply that they could overcome their pain if only they would try to get their minds off of it. Actually, my intention is somewhat different. I believe that with purpose and passion our ability to tolerate pain and stress is greatly increased. Such an abstraction might be hard to swallow while in the midst of pain but it is an extraordinary lesson to absorb as we plan our lives.

There is a great deal of overlap among a sense of purpose, a mission statement and one's personal identity. My first encounter with what having a *written* sense of purpose could mean occurred a few years ago when I visited a manufacturing company in middle Ohio. The company, Minster Stamping, located in Minster, Ohio, has a reputation for excellence in stamping out various shaped products. Their product was not my interest, however; an injured employee with chronic pain was the subject of my visit.

No sooner was I through the front door than I was met by a very cordial executive, greeting me warmly and handing me a laminated card. The card was the Minster Machine Company's Statement of Purpose. Now, as I write this some years later, I realize that it may sound somewhat hokey to be handing visitors a wallet-size card stating who you are. But no feeling of awkwardness was present on the day of the visit. The executive evidenced no measure of embarrassment over his action—he was proud of his company's identity and purpose and his position in it. He went over the statement of purpose with me.

On this little card was the assertion that the company was "founded, nurtured, and successfully built on the principles of integrity, quality and values by dedicated and spirited people." It stated a vision for the future and a mission detailing the specifics of how it was to be accomplished. It elaborated on those factors critical to its success and listed values that were the foundation for its quest of excellence—all on a card no bigger than a picture in your wallet. I was particularly impressed with the values cited:

* Honesty, trust and integrity
* Respect for each other
* Hard work with a "can do" attitude
* Team work
* Innovation and creativity

I was still trying to digest this opening exchange when I had to proceed with a tour of the facility and an extended interview with the injured worker and his co-workers. I can tell you, however, that the spirit of that little card stayed with me the rest of the day and it seemed to be present in every one of the men and women I encountered.

Perhaps I was naive on that day, for no one can adequately grasp the quality of an organization in a single visit. But I must tell you that I have visited many other companies, taken many tours, and met with many executives. None has made anything close to such a powerful impression. I felt that I knew with whom I was dealing and that "games" were not necessary. If the basis of relationship is trust, as I believe it is, than this company, with its purpose, mission and values clearly stated, had made giant strides in gaining my trust. From the first moment, they put their cards on the table, stated who they were and stood up tall. There was no ambiguity regarding their identity.

Have you ever viewed the Declaration of Independence at the Library of Congress in Washington, D.C.? The beauty and the power of the document is awesome. The Declaration of Independence can be considered a mission statement. It puts forth a statement of purpose, stating who we are ("We the People") and our goals:

"We hold these truths to be self-evident—that all men are created equal; that they are endowed by their Creator with certain inalienable rights; that among these are life, liberty, and the pursuit of happiness. That, to secure these rights, governments are instituted among men, deriving their just powers from the consent of the governed."

The Declaration of Independence, the Constitution and the Bill of Rights all spell out what we as a nation stand for. Each guides, directs, and tells others what we aspire to. We may not, in every moment, live up to those lofty standards but the nature of the standards tells something about us, something about our character.

When I tell an audience that I want them to work on a mission statement, I often hear a collective groan. Mission statements have become so commercialized that they have lost some of their meaning. In some instances, upper management dictates mission statements in the work place with little input or investment by the majority of the employees. This denies the mission statement any true meaning for it is the investment, the buy-in of the employees, that is the critical element. Without personal input into the creation of the mission statement, the words become meaningless. With honest contributions, with belief in the substance, mission statement can become a commitment to purpose. Throughout history, men and women have died for ideas, for statements of purpose.

We know that McDonald's makes fast food, Microsoft creates software, and Disney sells entertainment. What do you represent? What are the things that your life means? Earlier in the this chapter, you wrote out roles that you play, named people who are significant in your life and stated what you would like them to say at the end of your life. You considered what qualities you value. These qualities make up your character. They are the composite that is you. Now you can utilize them further by writing a statement of purpose, a personal statement of direction and goals.

Consider the following statement of resolution by Mahatma Gandhi:

> *"Let then our first act every morning be to make the*
> *following resolve for the day:*
> *I shall not fear anyone on earth.*
> *I shall fear only God.*
> *I shall not bear ill toward anyone.*
> *I shall not submit to injustice from anyone.*
> *I shall conquer untruth by truth.*
> *And in resisting untruth I shall put up with all suffering."*

Reading Gandhi's creed, there can be no question regarding his identity and principles. His direction in life was clear. And by daily stating his resolve, he reaffirmed his values and kept his focus clear.

Your statement need not be as extensive or as complicated as Gandhi's. The critical element is that it represents you and those goals you find meaningful. It can be as simple as, "My mission is to create an atmosphere in my family that enhances their growth and love for one another" or "My mission is to live in the moment, be kind, considerate and caring to others as well as myself and to continuously strive towards excellence." If you are moved by these words, then for you, that is the finest mission statement possible.

Mission statements are not necessarily permanent. They represent a statement of values, direction, aspirations and goals at a particular point in your life. Each of these variables can, and probably should, change. Certainly it is important to periodically review your direction in life. In that light, I encourage you not to be overly concerned with the finer points in the first draft of your mission statement. It is more important that you get a statement down on paper. You can fine-tune it at a later date. If few thoughts come to mind, return to your eulogy and examine the values and qualities that are present in your words. Consider those people and objectives that merited the most attention and perhaps you will find some ideas. Take the time right now to write out the first draft of your mission statement on the next page.

First Draft of My Mission Statement

Review the draft of your mission statement. Check to see if it inspires you. While it does not have to be earth shattering, it should make your pulse race just a little. "Wouldn't it be great? I would really be making a contribution. This is really worth striving for." These are the types of thoughts that emanate from meaningful mission statements. Even better are those mission statements that can be translated into tangible behaviors. If my mission statement involves enhancing the potential of people around me, I know that careful listening, along with support and encouragement, are the order of the day. If I take this mission statement to heart, placing it in a spot where it can prompt daily actions, the statement can become a real force in my life.

To some such an effort may sound silly. But it is worth noting that so many of the great men and women of the world became admirable, in large part, because they knew where they wanted to go and what they wanted to do. Surely, on perhaps a less grand scale, we too can live a life of purpose.

I commit myself to take care of myself for the sake of myself, my family, my friends, my community and my country.

Chapter 8

LISTENING, BEING GRATEFUL &

FORGIVING

A friend of mine who is a rehabilitation doctor recently told me the story of a patient she had been treating for a long time. It seems that the patient's chronic condition and particularly his chronic pain had improved as much as they were going to. After trying every test, therapy, and medication she could think of, the physician struggled to tell her patient that there was nothing more she could do and that perhaps he should seek other medical care. No sooner had the words left her mouth than the patient rushed to say that he too had known this was the case for a long time. But, he insisted that, while he respected her expertise, her medical knowledge was no longer his primary interest. It was the fact that she took the time to listen to him, giving him her full attention, which caused him to seek regular appointments. He assured her that her careful listening was not to be overlooked and, for his part, he had no intention of seeking other medical care.

I have been treating patients with serious physical conditions for twenty years. I'm sure it will not come as a surprise to hear that the complaint I hear most frequently regarding medical care is the lack of listening—this seemingly most simple of acts.

Courage, honesty, and perseverance may be the higher class qualities in the make-up of character, but listening, being grateful and forgiving are the quiet stars.

Take listening, for example. It is unfortunate that so little attention is given to this basic quality—a quality so very valuable in the experience of relationships. Think back to how listening is "learned" in childhood. If your memory is like mine, a child is being told to listen while they are being yelled at ("You pay attention when I'm talking to you"). Nowhere in my recollection is there a revered place for listening—a special admiration for this skill the way there is for bravery, loyalty or honesty.

Listening is special. To listen well is an extremely valuable asset. It allows you to enter into someone's world, to form a bonding unavailable to those who cannot or do not listen well. Its absence may be the cause of anger when we expect it to occur in potentially tense situations such as a doctor's office.

It is novel to some to even think of listening as a skill or quality of character, but the ability to listen well is most certainly a skill and one of the most valuable of those we can possess. To be able to listen well is to own an ability as valuable as any diamond.

Listening is deceptive. It appears easy and automatic, a passive behavior, but it is not. It takes energy, selflessness and certainly attention. To do it well takes sincerity and, at its highest form, empathy.

Poor listeners are legion—their minds racing ahead to what they wish to say. The worst of them, hardly maintain eye contact and interrupt, leaving the speaker with the empty feeling so often associated with disrespect.

The act of listening well is a gift for it also replenishes the speaker. Recall how you felt when your words were given full attention, when you were aware that the listener was completely occupied by your message. He didn't rush in to solve your problem, didn't assume you couldn't work it out, didn't give you advice—he just listened. What a gift. If you're like me, you felt validated and respected. You felt on equal footing with the listener and perhaps even closer because of the undivided, accepting attention given to your words. No, if you're a good listener, don't underestimate the value of your skill, you have a truly valuable asset—an asset which says a lot about your character.

You may be acquainted with the excellent book, The 7 *Habits of Highly Effective People,* written by Stephen Covey. Covey has acquired a well-deserved following for his message emphasizing organizational and personal change. As with many philosophies or world-views, there is a certain jargon that is acquired when one accepts the perspective of an author. In the language of *"7 Habits",* readers often speak of "paradigm shift," "win-win," "beginning with the end in mind"—concepts with which I encourage readers of this book to acquaint themselves by reading Covey's work.

I, along with a group of like minded health educators, recently met with a small business developer to seek basic information concerning the creation of a small enterprise. The developer, highly knowledgeable and very educated, was a devotee of Stephen Covey's work. His language was peppered with words revealing his attendance at Covey workshops. He was an expert—with one major failing. He failed to grasp Covey's Habit # 5, "Seek first to understand, then to be understood." He failed to listen. Here he was, with more knowledge in his area of expertise than the physician and psychologists in front of him, but all his knowledge failed to impress. We felt neither respected nor understood and he failed to establish the most basic of relationships. We consequently rushed to leave his office in spite of the services he could offer. Listening is indeed, basic, critical and a skill worth knowing.

I recently took a workshop on mediation—a procedure that has become increasingly popular in our legal system. Mediation is interesting in that it brings together what, by all appearances, are two irreconcilable points of view. For example, one side may contend that their neighbor's dog has been barking all night, disturbing their sleep. Despite repeated polite requests to the neighbor to quiet the dog, their sleep continues to be interrupted by incessant barking. The dog owner, for his part, sees his dog as necessary for security and also a faithful companion—two very opposing points of view. How could mediation reconcile these two polar positions?

The process and the concept is quite simple although it often requires a skilled mediator. What the mediator does, however, is not arbitrate or judge. Quite the contrary. The role of the mediator is to get the participants to clearly state their point of view, citing all relevant information and conditions. The mediator draws out as full a statement of facts and feelings from each party as possible. And here is the critical piece—the opposing parties have to listen. They have to listen carefully because each party has to come up with a solution acceptable to *both* parties. In this example, the issues of both safety and sleep would have to be heard and addressed.

In most conflicts very little listening occurs. The immediate response in most arguments is the creation of defenses, the hardening of positions and certainly the shutdown of listening. The heart of mediation is getting both parties to *really* listen to one another.

What happens when listening occurs? Perceptions often change. Oh, not immediately because personal biases can be strong. But with increased listening, we begin to hear details not originally in our understanding. We begin to see the circumstances and the conditions present for the other person's actions. And most importantly, we come to see the other person as a human being. Mediation establishes a framework so that the simple act of listening can occur.

Listening is magical. It brings us into awareness that we all share fears, anxieties, worries and feelings. It can heal. No one who is able to listen well is without character.

BEING GRATEFUL

A Rehabilitation Psychology friend tells the story of a quadriplegic patient he had treated for a long time. In the course of therapy, my friend asked this man what he would wish for if he could ask God for anything at all. The man, with no hesitation, said that he would wish to be a "para"—that is, a paraplegic. Surprised at the patient's answer, the psychologist responded: "No, no, you can have anything. You can have full functioning with all your limbs in your wish." "Oh, I understand," replied the patient. "But I don't want to ask God for too much and I would be quite happy with the use of just two of my limbs."

This story jolts us into a new perspective. It illustrates how happiness is a relative matter and how our outlook plays a critical role in our well-being. But it also demonstrate the importance of appreciating those gifts, experiences, relationships we do have.

It is interesting to read the research comparing people who perceive themselves as happy compared with those who don't. One finding that stands out is the sensitivity of happy people to the little things in life. Their antennae are tuned-in to those everyday experiences that others allow to pass by—not only a pleasant smile, the smell of food, the warmth of the sun but small pleasantries and kindness, the fortunes of relative health and the goodness of others.

Raising sensitivity to the complexities of life and to its subtle pleasures can be valuable. With this intention, I often begin workshops with an exercise in which participants are asked to assume that they are beginning their life anew. With the choice of one new life to live and carrying with them their current values, workshop participants are asked to choose from alternatives that include both positive and negative features. Some of the alternatives from this exercise are listed below. Read them over and consider what choice you might make. Remember you have to choose one from the list below. This is a real clarification of values.

WOULD YOU CHOOSE TO...

1. Be a tremendously popular politician who has little sense of integrity?
2. Make a wonderful contribution to humanity but have your most hated enemy receive full credit for your accomplishments?
3. Create happiness for the people you love but still maintain a severe depression throughout your life?
4. Be a renowned, self assured, confident psychologist with no arms nor legs?
5. Be a famous actress or actor, fabulously wealthy, but never in a solid personal relationship?
6. Be a great leader but live your life in constant and severe poverty?

7. Be a fabulously successful business tycoon who is not trusted by anyone?

8. Be a coal miner in South Africa, working in dirty and harsh conditions, but with a loving and caring family?

9. Be a self-assured, confident person who was born with a grossly disfigured face?

10. Be a brilliant scientist who has a severely disabling muscular disorder?

11. Live in a loving, secure family and home but be mentally retarded?

12. Live a saintly life, devoutly religious, but sequestered in a monastery?

13. Have wonderful powers of serenity but be unjustly imprisoned for life?

As you read the alternatives, you may not have wanted to choose any of them. Each carries a significant burden. So the choice become which alternative is tolerable and provides a benefit which is most valued. If you seriously consider the alternatives and reflect upon the choice made, the personal qualities you most value are illuminated.

The purpose of this exercise is to raise sensitivity regarding each person's values and to increase the awareness that we all carry a mixture of attributes and burdens. The exercise has prompted many respondents to put their own positive and negative experience into perspective. I have expanded this analysis by asking each person to create their own list, made up of people they know, including themselves. The task is to examine lives in terms of their best attributes or fortunes coupled with the heaviest burden they have had to carry. Typically a respondent comes up with a list such as the following:

1. A very successful man who hides deep feelings of insecurity and depression.

2. A woman who is kind and gentle but bore a child with Down Syndrome and whose own parents were tragically killed in an automobile accident.
3. A woman of great beauty who has repeatedly been abused in her relationships.
4. A basically good man whose social skill are so poor that he lives most of his life feeling lonely and isolated.

These examples are not unusual. They represent a cross section of people that we all know and would probably be similar to a list any of us would make. Each of us has attributes of which we could be proud. But we are also likely to carry burdens, suffering, hardships. It is the person who understands that life is made up of this mixture, with periods in which the balance seems unjust, who appears to cope well. If such an outlook is coupled with an appreciation of life's smaller pleasantries, life becomes all the more positive.

I recently visited my daughter in Atlanta. She has a ritual before dinner each evening of giving thanks for three events that happened during the course of her day. Such a practice helps to put life's challenges into perspective. It elevates awareness of our fortune, creates awareness for the daily sharing of positive experiences with our family and fights the tendency to become overwhelmed by difficult experiences. I'm trying to follow her good example.

FORGIVENESS

One of the most charitable and forgiving acts ever recorded occurred in 1994—a cruel, senseless act was followed by a response sublime in character. The crime was a random drive-by shooting of Nicholas Green, a 7-year-old-child who was visiting Italy with his parents. Driving on a highway, these parents witnessed their child's life wrenched from their family.

No Italian hearing of this atrocity would deny these American parents a response of rage and bitterness, or thoughts of revenge. What the Italians witnessed instead from the parents was kindness, understanding and forgiveness. Instead of acting out of rancor and hatred, quite understandable in such a moment of horror, the parents donated all their son's organs to Italians in need. The Italians were so overwhelmed by this response of giving in the face of anguish that they in turn increased their own organ donation by 25%.

Two years later, following the trial of two men accused of the shooting (There were no witnesses and the men were found innocent), the parents returned to Italy to throngs of admiring crowds, a school named after their son and seven Italians who now shared their son's organs.

The response of Nicholas' parents is extraordinary for many, many reasons. When most of us are hurt by others we tend to become defensive, angry, and resentful. These are common responses, almost automatic. Nicholas's parents chose another response—one that calls on character of the highest order—forgiveness.

Forgiveness is not the same as condoning or excusing nor is it reconciliation. It is a virtue difficult to achieve but filled with benefits—for the alternative, holding onto hate, spite and hostility, is corrosive to the mind, body and soul. Carrying such feelings is clearly associated with a number of health problems, but the mental burden may be even greater. Feelings of hate take enormous energy, distort reality, and prohibit growth.

Forgiveness releases the poison, allowing life to move forward. It facilitates a reduction of depression and anxiety and frees the mind to return to a fuller life. It acknowledges circumstances but does not excuse. Most importantly, it returns a measure of control to the victim. Forgiveness can change a life.

I recall a patient I had been seeing for depression for some time who left a message that he was going to miss an appointment. When I saw this usually quite depressed man on his next visit, I was surprised by his very upbeat positive demeanor. When I asked the source of his pleasure, he told me that his father had died. Before I could ask how his father dying could be the cause of his pleasure, he quickly informed me that he and his father had held lifetime grudges against one another. They had not spoken for years over issues now even difficult to accurately recall. Since his previous appointment, he and his father, who was gravely ill, had met. They listened carefully to one another, cried and forgave each other for past transgressions. My patient told me that I could not imagine how much "lighter" he felt. He could not recall feeling this way for years. Yes, it was sad that all those years had been wasted and he truly grieved over the loss of his father. But he wanted me to know that he felt so incredibly fortunate that he forgave and was forgiven by his father.

MY SHORTEST SESSION EVER

It was about 8:45 A.M. and I sat in my office, with the door open, completing some paperwork. My first appointment was for 9 A.M. but I noticed out of the corner of my eye a middle-aged woman who had left the waiting area and who was not too subtly checking me out. Since my paperwork could be completed later, I asked my secretary if the woman outside my office was my first patient and she informed me that it was. My secretary commonly guides new patients to the office and introduces them to me. I, in turn, introduce myself and welcome the patient. On this morning my introduction was met with a stony silence and a very hostile glare. After perhaps 20 mute seconds, the patient said in a clipped, deliberate fashion, "I don't like you." Taken aback by her aggressive tone, I inquired as to why she felt this dislike. Continuing her glare, she spit out the words, "You're a psychologist. You think you can read people's minds." And with that she got up and abruptly left my office.

I've had many patients like this woman—people so filled with anger toward others that they are ready to explode. When the anger is directed toward me, I attempt to explain that I am not able to read anyone's mind and thereby provide an immediate solution to his problem. What I am able to do is to sincerely listen to them and offer them some services that they are free to choose or reject.

I feel sorry for individuals who are consumed with intense anger. These individuals or patients are caught in a most deceptive trap, believing that their troubles and frustrations are overwhelmingly due to others. It is understandable how such a belief can come about. It is very easy to direct our frustration outward and point a finger to a single cause. While it is a common experience to feel unjustly treated, it is self-destructive to maintain such an attitude for any length of time. When any of us continue to believe that our suffering and misery are caused by others, we give up the very control needed to help resolve the problem.

The woman in this example had chronic pain, an intensely difficult problem to manage. In all likelihood she had seen a number of physicians, one or several of whom may have told her that her pain was "all in her head." She may have had a bad experience with a psychiatrist or psychologist. Relatives or friends may have ridiculed her or themselves had bad experiences.

In the field of therapy there are incredibly wonderful therapists who are caring, sensitive, patient and professional. There are also individuals who are the clear opposite of each one of these virtues. The same can be said of virtually every occupation. Humans come in all variations. However, when we blame our woes on others, we are prone to irrational thinking. At these moments, looking inward and searching for our own qualities of tolerance and forgiveness can be most effective.

You might be interested to know that psychologists pay relatively little for malpractice insurance—typically $400 to $800 annually, a tiny fraction of what most physicians pay. You might argue that psychologists cannot inflict the harm that a physician potentially can with improper medications or surgery, so the much smaller insurance premium seems reasonable. I would argue that such an argument is only partially true, for psychologist are dealing with the most intense of suffering— emotional pain. They are dealing with patients when they are most vulnerable and therefore subject to great harm. They are hearing inner secrets, intimate fears, and anxieties— often hidden from all other humans. Improper psychotherapeutic intervention can (and sometimes does) cause great damage. But why then do psychologists not pay enormous sums for malpractice insurance? The answer is simple. The stock and trade of clinical psychologists is listening, empathizing and accepting—basic and critical elements in the creation of trust. Without doubt, rules and commitment to confidentially also play a substantial role, but it is sincere listening, empathizing and accepting which lead to a trusting relationships—and trust is the antithesis of litigation.

The research literature has been clear that malpractice litigation is not simply a result of improper procedures, for all professionals make errors of judgement. In the majority of situations, the critical coexisting condition is the failure to establish a trusting relationship.

It would be wonderful to claim many of the qualities previously listed in this book—courage, bravery, perseverance, honesty, integrity, charity, loyalty, honor, and so forth. But you might consider three of the lessor known "stars" and proudly add them to your list—the ability to listen well, being grateful for what you have and the capacity to forgive.

As you end the first section of this book with its emphasis upon character it's a good time to repeat the exercise performed in Chapter 2. You will recall that exercise as asking a friend to give you their nonjudgmental, uninterrupted attention for four minutes while you describe yourself. On this second occasion, see if you can incorporate some of the qualities that are the make-up of your character. Consider the following list of qualities that have been mentioned in this book:

Honest	Reliable
Honorable	Respectful
Person of Integrity	Forgiving
Hard Worker	Kind
Persevering	Brave
Sincere	Conscientious
Trustworthy	Charitable
Good Humored	Good Listener
Optimistic	Resourceful
Caring	Loyal
Grateful	Sensitive

You may think of some additional ones not on the list. Circle those that apply to you and include as many as you can in your second four-minute description of yourself. Remember these qualities are you—they are your treasures.

Once again I ask that you have this exchange with a friend. You ask your friend to listen attentively without interruptions for four minutes as you describe yourself and then, in turn, you give the same courtesy to your friend.

If you have also selected possible models, written a eulogy and a mission statement, you have identified many descriptions that can influence your personal narrative.

I commit myself to take care of myself for the sake of myself, my family, my friends, my community and my country.

Section Two

POLISHING THE INNER CORE

Chapter 9

SELF-ESTEEM

JANET was twenty-nine years old, married for eleven years and the mother of two children, ages six and eight. Her husband was an automobile parts salesman who owned his own business and made a good living. On the surface, their lives had many of the features of a happy American family. However, Janet had unrelenting headaches for ten years, which she described as an intense tension at the base of her skull radiating over the top of her head to her forehead. She had been to many physicians, tried innumerable medications, had several teeth extracted, wore a mouth splint and various other appliances to reduce concurrent nocturnal bruxism (teeth grinding). She claimed that she had not had a day without pain for ten years.

When we saw Janet, pain was clearly written on her face. Just as notable was the slight forward thrust of her shoulders. This modification of her trapezium (the massive muscle of the upper back and shoulders that extends over much of the skull) created an intense tightness. Imagine holding any muscle rigid for all of one's waking hours (and given the patient's nocturnal teeth grinding patterns, probably through the sleeping hours as well), and you can imagine the tension in her upper back, neck and head. All previous attempts (e.g., biofeedback, relaxation training and physical therapy) had failed to relieve this patient's muscular tension and her headaches.

A major clue as to the source of Janet's muscular tension became apparent during an interview with the patient and her husband. She was extremely passive, an intense "pleaser," and terrified of making an error. Her children and her house were immaculate at all times. She had the proverbial floor that one could eat off. She was small in stature with downcast eyes and a soft voice. Her husband, on the other hand, was large, strong appearing and rough in his presentation. He, a former marine sergeant, was demanding in his voice and tone and aggressive in his speech. The couple, so opposite in appearance, professed a strong marital bond and denied any marital conflict. It was readily apparent, however, that Janet "walked on eggs" each and every day. In the process, she had learned to hold her muscles in a tense, rigid manner. Hence her constant headaches.

The answer to relieving this patient's headaches appears very straightforward—have the patient and her husband go into marriage counseling. Life, however, is not so simple. Janet's husband would not tolerate any suggestion that he enter counseling.

Many audiences, on hearing this case study, have suggested a more aggressive answer to relieving Janet's headaches—"Get rid of her husband." Again, life is not so simple. Janet was totally dependent on her husband for her own and her children's financial security. She had known no other man, and he was the father of their children. She professed intense love for him. Most importantly, Janet's self-esteem was incredibly poor. In only one area did she show any independence and firmness. When asked if her husband had ever physically abused her, this meek, slight woman straightened up and said with determination, "I told him when he proposed marriage that, if he ever hit me, he better not close his eyes at night, because he would not wake up in the morning." And upon completing that statement, she, like a turtle pulling in its neck, returned to her passive state.

It is important to note that even if Janet did separate from her husband, the probability is great that she would remarry in a short time to a man who would dominate her and she would continue to be a "pleaser." On the surface, the source of the tension appears to be the overbearing, critical style of the husband. In the broader picture, the heart of the difficulty was extremely poor self-esteem. She was helpless to stand up for herself and held all her tension in her muscles.

Janet represents an extreme case of poor self-esteem, but illustrates the devastating effect that such a personal outlook can have on a life. What exactly is self-esteem? "It is how we perceive ourselves." This straightforward answer is consistently given and is right on the mark. How we think about ourselves is the foundation of what is referred to as our self-esteem. It is a generalization, a perception, a feeling that we have concerning our values, abilities and our sense of who we are. Self-esteem is one of the critical things we own but to which we pay little heed. Most people accept their self-esteem passively. It is not one of those things very susceptible to change and not something we concern ourselves with. It just is. I don't agree with this attitude and would like to share an alternative view.

The subject of self-esteem is particularly interesting in a rehabilitation setting. Working in such an atmosphere provides the opportunity to not only observe severe physical limitations but to see the incredible fortitude exhibited by many of the rehabilitation residents. In a rehabilitation setting it is possible on any given day to see patients with extraordinary disabilities who will meet you with a smile, a sense of humor and a clear sense of who they are. One such man I knew lived in a long-term rehabilitation facility for many years at the end of his life. Physically he was only half a man, literally not existing from the waist down. He transported himself on a flat cart, positioning himself in a prone arrangement and propelling himself with his arms. I never knew this man to be without a smile, an upbeat remark and a confident air. I may be confusing optimism with self-confidence but I would wager this physically disabled man's self-esteem was very good.

We can find many such individuals if we would only look—the one-legged skier, the wheelchair marathoner, the one-armed baseball player. Several years ago, a blind sailor navigated half way around the world totally by himself. There are thousands of severely disabled individuals who go to work everyday, have families and are exemplary citizens of our country. Such extraordinary accomplishments come about because these individuals have a sense of who they are that allows them to expand their horizons. They come from a foundation that is solid and not tarnished by continuous self-doubts, although they, like the best of us, have occasional episodes. They have overcome the temptation to continuously feel sorry for themselves or blame others or "the world" for their disability. We need to do more than admire their tenacity and courage. We need to examine their belief system and their self-esteem and work to match those perceptions in our own lives.

Where does our self-esteem come from? Surely we are not born with a perception of who we are. This generalization is established during our childhood and probably most influenced by our parents or the adults providing parenting attention. I often ask audiences to assume that they are given the responsibility of a new born child and to decide to give their child a most precious gift—good self-esteem. How would they go about it? The answers typically start off with "love, caring and security" to which I reply affirmatively but ask for a more precise statement of parenting behaviors. The reply then becomes, "Give the child praise and attention." "How much?" I reply. "As much as possible," comes the answer. This is an interesting response and one that has been well researched. Most parents and teachers believe that they provide their children and students with ample praise. Research says otherwise. Parents and teachers have been found to consistently overestimate the quantity of praise given their charges. But the audience is correct in noting the importance of providing positive reinforcement.

Not only do we often overestimate the frequency of our praise but we tend to overestimate our ability in giving praise. The inability to give compliments appears evident when I assign family members the task of praising their chronic pain relatives during a family therapy class. Repeatedly, adult's fumble, show embarrassment and typically give very general statements. To make matters worse, poor eye contact and low volume are most common.

I was once asked by a hospital employee how he might improve his relationship with his misbehaving eleven-year-old daughter. Given the circumstance of choosing one quick recommendation in a hospital corridor, I suggested that he give his child ten positive remarks every day and move away from his emphasis on her *mis*behavior. He came back in a week telling me that my recommendation was useless. I was surprised at his remark, given the usual success of this recommendation and asked him to describe a typical compliment. He stated, with some frustration that just last night at the dinner table he had informed his daughter that she was "finally not eating like a pig." So much for good praising skills.

In the family therapy session we teach adults the tools of praising, good eye contact, a firm sincere voice, and spelling out of specific behavior. Not "good work", but "wonderful job with your exercise. You really look like you've got the hang of it." Not stated as if you were reading an instruction manual but with enthusiasm, the way you would like a similar remark expressed to you. The goal is to build a new belief system, a belief system built with substantive "bricks"—bricks that can be relied upon. This is the process effective parents and teachers use. They further enhance the effectiveness of their praise by building a bridge between compliments. Not only is Johnny "caught" doing a wonderful job of cleaning the yard, but his yard cleaning skills are coupled with his other abilities. "Johnny, what a great job you did with the yard. I especially like the way you trimmed the edge. You're very creative. You're a neat kid." Every opportunity is taken to provide Johnny with abundant praise and in particular to build a generalization within Johnny's head—"Yes indeed, I am a 'neat' kid, who is worthwhile, a part of this family and who can do many things." Building good self-esteem requires an avalanche of such thoughts.

Reality dictates that not all childhood behavior can be followed by praise. Some of what children do is destructive, harmful, and mischievous. Children need to be provided instruction and guidance in order to acquire the ability to deal effectively with a complex world. It is inefficient to wait for positive actions to occur in order for the child to learn. This is where corrective parenting comes in—correcting the behaviors and not criticizing the child. This is the gold standard that we can seek to reach. The wealth of research and the authority of the child psychology field stands behind the axiom, "Correct the behavior, don't punish the child."

In order to effectively teach we need to provide the child with information so that the future action can be improved. Punishing the child does little in the teaching of a healthy,

positive self-esteem. When, for example, the child is ridiculed ("Can't you do anything right" or "Only a dummy
couldn't figure that out"), we are building poor self-esteem
and buttressing the belief that the child is inferior. On the
other hand, when a mistake is made and instructions are
given or behavior is modeled for the child, we build skills
and cement relationships. The idea is straightforward. Create a constructive atmosphere for the nurturing of a positive
self-esteem. Do everything possible to praise and support
the creation of the generalization that the child is a worthwhile, capable individual who is able to withstand the challenges of life. Help the child to acquire a perception that
errors are a part of life that exists in the learning process and
are not a reflection of his inadequacies. Teach the child to
be kind and *compassionate with himself* as well as others.

The interesting point of the above discussion is how
often patients and my audiences agree with the common
sense nature of the contentions. I don't believe I have ever
heard anyone disagree with the proposition that children
should be praised. Some may dispute my argument that parental punishment should be avoided whenever possible
but, even on these grounds, general consensus is the norm.
However the next matter is more problematic. After all this
agreement, I ask the question **"Do you do the same for yourself?"** Are you abundant with praise toward yourself? Do you
search out areas of accomplishment? Is your "antennae" sensitive to positives more then negatives? Are you willing to
consider your own errors as part of the learning process rather
a measure of yourself? Can you allow yourself the same kindness and compassion you would provide to a child? If the
answer to these questions is less than a vigorous yes, I recommend the work on your self-esteem.

It appears self evident that good self-esteem is a desirable goal. Certainly the goal of a constantly developing and
improving self-esteem has much merit. In a marvelous little

book entitled, *How To Be Your Own Best Friend,* Newman, M &
Berkowitz, B. remind us that:

> *"It is up to us to give ourselves recognition. If we wait*
> *for it to come from others, we feel resentful when it*
> *doesn't, and when it does, we may well reject it. It is*
> *not what others say to us that counts. We all love*
> *praise, but have you ever noticed how quickly the glow*
> *from a compliment wears off? When we compliment*
> *ourselves, the compliment stays with us. It is still good*
> *to hear from others, but it doesn't matter so much if we*
> *have already heard it from ourselves. This is the trag-*
> *edy of some marvelous performers, who need endless*
> *applause to tell them how great they are, but who feel a*
> *chill as soon as they enter their dressing rooms. They*
> *have never heard it from themselves."* [52]

Assuming that we accept the goal of improving our self-esteem we need to establish a plan. The first step is to define
what we mean by good self-esteem. I would define a person
with good self-esteem as one who:

A) Processes information in a manner that is construc-
    tive to his well-being.
B) Is in touch with his positive values and characteris-
    tics and
C) Has a stable positive perception of himself in the
    face of criticism or adversity.

Let's take each one of these specific aspects and examine it more closely. The first, processing information in a
manner that is constructive to one's well being, simply means
that we use the information around us in a beneficial way. In
reality most individuals do not. A good model illustrating
this point was put forward over thirty years ago by Maxwell

Maltz, in his excellent self-help book, *Psychocybernetics.* Maltz proposed that when it comes to processing information, we should use a cybernetics model such as a rocket. A rocket is energized with a goal "in mind." Assuming that the rocket is heat seeking, it then seeks feedback (in this case, heat) which allows it to get closer to its goal (target). Each bit of positive feedback (heat information) is processed toward the end of reaching the goal ("I'm getting closer to my goal"). When negative information ("I'm off course") is obtained, the rocket utilizes that knowledge to get back on course. No self-incriminations are added, no generalizations concerning the rocket's inadequacies are generated. Positive information is used to move closer to the goal. Negative information is used to move closer to the goal.

Do most people actively seek positive feedback? Most people avoid such action. We have been well conditioned to restrict any conspicuous effort that appears as if we are soliciting a compliment. The conditioning process begins early with social sanctions such as "Don't get big headed" or "You're getting too big for your britches." These sanctions are commonplace and have the decided effect of inhibiting overt attempts to seek positive feedback. The end result is that for most of us, a strong sense of anticipated humiliation is associated with seeking positive feedback.

Juxtaposed with the avoidance of overtly seeking positive feedback is the fear of being criticized. Indeed, most of us are guided more by the possibility of being criticized than the prospect of receiving a compliment. It is commonplace to passively hope for positive feedback (praise) and actively avoid negative feedback (criticism). This pattern is incredibly harmful to the development of good self-esteem.

If we examine the process within a person who has poor self-esteem, the deficiencies of the practice becomes even more evident. Imagine a young man with poor self-esteem. You might be able to recognize him by his poor posture, eye contact and carriage. Now visualize him walking down the hall when someone appears to give him a "dirty look." How do you think he interprets this negative information? Most likely, he internalizes it, wonders what he has done wrong, or believes that the person doesn't like him. In other words he takes a small amount of negative information, exaggerates it and allows the event to further contribute to a damaged self-esteem.

On another occasion the same person may walk down the hall, this time receiving a compliment such as "nice shirt." The person with poor self-esteem has a high likelihood of deflecting the compliment, perhaps even totally distorting it. "He didn't really mean that" or "What is he after?" would be common interpretations. Negative information is expanded and typically distorted while positive information is deflated and devalued. If the cybernetics rocket followed the pattern of the person with poor self-esteem we can only imagine its course. As it strays off course and receives information to that effect, it says to itself, "What an idiot rocket I am, no other rocket is as stupid as I am." And with that it crashes.

Compare the above process with a person who has good self-esteem. Again we can visualized the person walking down the hall. This time, however, with good posture, eye contact and carriage. Imagine someone appearing to give our good self-esteem person a dirty look. Undeterred, our good self-esteem person is probably not bothered by the actions of others to the same degree as our poor self-esteem friend. For he is unlikely to personalize the dirty look, unlikely to mind read the critical expression and unlikely to focus on the scowl. Instead our good self-image person is likely to deflect the look by interpreting it as someone else's problem—"He's having a bad day"; "I wonder what's going on with him"; "Boy did he get up on the wrong side of the bed." Notice the lack of overgeneralization of the negative. The incident is kept tight, a minor occurrence in the course of the day.

Examine the same individual walking down the hall but this time receiving a compliment, such as "nice shirt". Our self-confident friend takes this remark in with comfort, no resistance, no depreciation, and no negative distortion. If anything, our friend tends to generalize the positive, thinking—"Yes, it's true this is a nice shirt. I have good taste in shirts and in clothes in general." Observe self-confident individuals, notice how frequently they compliment themselves.[53] Little remarks, build, maintain and develop a positive self-esteem.

Contrast the same events with good and poor self-esteem individuals. With positive remarks, the poor self-esteem person undermines the remark while the good self-esteem person tends to magnify it. With negative remarks the poor self-esteem person tends to magnify and distort while the good self-esteem person is likely to diminish their importance. Our friend with good self-esteem processes information closer to the cybernetics model and is also being more compassionate with himself.

The processing of information in a manner that is *detrimental* to the well being of the person was well illustrated in a patient we treated a few years ago.

Seventeen-year-old Darrell had been referred to us from Children's Hospital with a diagnosis of chronic and severe headaches that, according to the patient, had been present as long as he could remember. The headaches had been so severe that he missed 30 days of his junior year of high school and his entire senior year. Darrell was very overweight, quite shy, somewhat effeminate and generally passive. He also had a severe case of acne. Such a condition was ripe for mean taunts from his classmates. His home environment, too, was not conducive to the building of good self-esteem. Both his older sister and morbidly obese mother (i.e., 470 pounds) were on social security disability for health reasons and his father was extremely overprotective. With this background, this sad young man found his only refuge and reinforcement in the act of the caretaking for his very young and presumably non-critical siblings.

Critical to both the understanding and the treatment of this young man's chronic pain syndrome was his incredibly poor self-esteem. He could barely think of a positive thing to say about himself when directly asked. When given any type of compliment, he would immediately disavow it. It was easy to find abundant compliments to give him. He was quite bright, had excellent interpersonal skills and was obviously kind and caring. Each compliment, however, was followed by the reply, "I've heard that before; it doesn't mean anything." It was initially almost impossible to penetrate his armor of negativity. Only after a two-week avalanche of compliments from the staff and his fellow patients, coupled with direct evidence of the veracity of the praise, did some change occur.

Darrell is a good example of how the ineffective processing of information maintains poor self-esteem. He was hypersensitive to information that supported his perceptions of inadequacy and almost impervious to evidence recognizing excellence. And he was prone to overgeneralizations ("This is always happening to me, I can't do anything right").

What is also lacking in Darrell and others with poor self-esteem is perspective. Each lacks an awareness that they have survived previous setbacks and may have even handled them well. Processing information well means, in part, the ability to put current issues in perspective. It is useful to learn from Darrell's mistake. If we are to process information in a constructive fashion it is important that potentially harmful and upsetting experiences are considered in the light of useful past information. Make sure you are aware of your own strengths in surviving life's problems. Prepare yourself for future setbacks by writing out those challenges that you have survived or may have handled well. Take a few moments to complete the exercise on the next page.

THINGS I HAVE HANDLED WELL OR HAVE

MANAGED TO SURVIVE

1.

2.

3.

4.

5.

Keep your list of those challenges in life that you have managed to survive in a handy place to be available at the time of a new difficulty. When you are at the bottom of a mountain fretting over the steepness of the climb, you may forget that you have often been at the bottom of other mountains. Remember you can't climb a mountain unless you start at the bottom and that you've climbed other mountains from a similar place.

Awareness of those challenges that you have overcome is only half of perspective. The other half is the sensitivity to those positive events that have occurred in your life. To help gain perspective concerning life's pleasures, I commend that you keep a "Smile File." Create a file of positive events, experiences, commendations, supportive letters, awards and achievements. When someone gives you a compliment that you particularly value, write it down on a piece of paper, date it , and store it for future benefit. Save thank you notes you receive that particularly touch you. And, when you feel low and unappreciated, read the evidence of the many times in your life when you have been both successful and appreciated—and know that you will again.

A few years ago, I went to Epcot Center at Disney World. Within that fascinating setting, there is a nostalgic theme restaurant, called *The Good Times Cafe*. Set in the 1950's, the furnishings, the menu, the requirement by the waitress that I wash my hands before I would be served, all brought back an incredible emotional recollection. You do a similar thing when you open a family album, not only seeing the pictures of familiar people and places, but bringing back the emotions tied to those thoughts. I recommend that you systematically do the same thing regarding positive events in your life. If you are to maintain a good mental ecology, it is worthwhile to do the work of mining the "memory gold" of the past and storing it for those times when you need it. Don't wait until the moments of anguish when the problem makes your ability to put things into perspective more difficult. My personal smile file is filled with letters from former patients, compliments from friends I've not seen in many years and things that I pride. It is difficult for me to maintain a negative perspective or to be overwhelmed when I have this file in front of me. One additional point. Within this bounty of positive memories, I have placed one item that reminds me of just how bad things can be, an object that stirs my memory to a time in my life when I was at my lowest ebb, a time that I have survived. Between my positives and a memory of a major event that I have overcome, I can't help but put my current problem in perspective.

Smile File

A Smile File is a collection of materials that bring back positive memories and is to be used to put inconveniences, failings and sad periods of your life into perspective.

Example of items which might be placed in your supportive file:

Letters from friends	Awards you have received
Thank you notes received for kindness you have done	Public recognition you have received (e.g., your name in the newspaper, etc.)
Compliments from others	Statement(s) of promotions
Your list of positive characteristics	Handicaps you have overcome
Inspirational statements that are particularly meaningful to you.	Difficulties that you have worked through
Lists of accomplishments which you are proud	Pictures that remind you of important friends, relatives or events.

Keep your "Smile File" handy for those days in life that are hard.

Processing information constructively and putting life's problems in perspective is the first part of good self-esteem. My definition of good self-esteem also includes being in touch with positive values and characteristics. In an interesting demonstration that illustrates the difference between individuals with poor and good self-esteem, I often ask a group of patients or an audience to tell me their positive characteristics.

Take a moment and respond to this question yourself. On the next page, write down your positive characteristics and negative characteristics, skills or traits.

LIST YOUR POSITIVE AND NEGATIVE

CHARACTERISTICS, SKILLS OR TRAITS

Positive Characteristics	Negative Characteristics
1.	1.
2.	2.
3.	3.
4.	4.
5.	5.
6.	6.
7.	7.

People with poor self-esteem are often speechless in response to questions concerning their positive characteristics. To dramatize their response, I overtly look at my watch, and often wait 20 or 30 seconds before hearing a single utterance. I am genuinely sorry and profusely apologize for putting anyone on the spot, but the illustration can be both startling and beneficial. Individuals with poor self-esteem are unaccustomed to even thinking of themselves in a positive vein.

In those individuals with poor self-esteem, characteristics frequently appear of a serving, helping or pleasing nature. "I'm a good mother, cook, or housekeeper" are examples of what I'm referring to. I do not mean to diminish the value of these behaviors. With few exceptions, however, I find that when a person is primarily dependent on service to others to gauge their self-worth, the potential for weakness is significant. It is the combination of an inability to sense our own positive characteristics and then to be *primarily* reliant on behaviors that warrant others' approval that appears particularly problematic.

It is interesting to note that poor self-esteem has little to do with talent or ability. It is purely a belief, a generalization regarding oneself. Endless examples of extremely self-deprecating people who have accomplished extraordinary deeds can be made. Indeed, a case can be made that the neurotic striving to achieve is often built upon a feeling of inadequacy. Many great men and women and their deeds support such an interpretation. John Quincy Adams is just one of thousands of such examples.

In his mid-life John Quincy Adams wrote in his diary:

> *"I am forty-five years old. Two-thirds of a long life have passed, and I have done nothing to distinguish it by usefulness to my country and to mankind."*

This is a man who held the following offices: Minister to the Hague, Emissary to England, Minister to Prussia, State Senator, United States Senator, Minister to Russia, Head of the American Mission to negotiate peace with England, Minister to England, Secretary of State, member of the House of Representatives and President of the United States. And yet close to his death at age eighty, John Quincy Adams wrote somberly in his diary that:

> *"(My) whole life has been a succession of disappointments. I can scarcely recollect a single instance of success in anything I have ever undertook."*[54]

The motivation to strive for extraordinary achievement is often energized by the wish to prove the belief of inadequacy wrong. While monumental accomplishments are the outcome for some, they come at a cost of incredible personal suffering. And there are the millions who never accomplish a fraction of their potential because of their endless self-deprecation.

Notice in the example of the young patient, Darrell, that it was not simply his inability to come up with positive self-statements, it was his inability to believe those thoughts and perceptions. He could repeatedly be told how bright he was only to dismiss the compliment. Only by "hammering" his inaccurate perceptions with contradictions ("Is it really true that you can't do anything right?") and have him substantiate the accuracy of more constructive beliefs ("I guess it is true that I'm smart. I did get the highest grade in my literature class.") was it possible for change to begin. He was consistently challenged in his self-destructive perceptions and persistently supported to search and seek the abundant evidence for a positive self-esteem.

Self-esteem is a combination of the thoughts and attitudes a person has towards himself. A person with good self-esteem has the ability to be sensitive to thoughts of self-worth, and to know either implicitly or explicitly, that there is substance behind these observations.

Interestingly enough, most people do not deny favorable attributes once they are brought to their attention (through recognition). As mentioned earlier, most people with poor self-esteem have a difficult time *recalling* their positive characteristics, skills and traits, even when the characteristics are clearly present. I enjoy questioning my audiences about whether they possess the characteristics espoused in the Boy Scout Creed. Do you possess these characteristic? Are you honest, trustworthy, loyal, helpful, friendly, courteous, kind, obedient, cheerful, thrifty, brave, clean and reverent. Most of us would be hard pressed to deny most of these characteristics. In all fairness, the characteristics mentioned need only be present the majority of the time. No one is totally honest throughout his life, perfectly kind, courteous and cheerful, etc. These are behaviors that simply need to be prominent the majority of the time, not 100% of the time.

Take the time to examine the list of positive and negative characteristics listed on the next two pages. Consider which of the characteristics are true of you most of the time. Circle those attributes and behaviors and then compare the list with those characteristics you listed earlier in this chapter.

CHOOSE YOUR POSITIVE CHARACTERISTICS FROM THE FOLLOWING LIST: CIRCLE THOSE ADJECTIVES THAT ARE APPLICABLE TO YOU MOST OF THE TIME

trustworthy	honest	faithful	kind
creative	articulate	sensitive	courteous
optimistic	neat	clean	caring
responsible	thoughtful	assertive	civic-minded
intelligent	conscientious	determined	persistent
patient	insightful	fit	dependable
imaginative	reliable	interesting	warm
socially aware	believable	organized	polite
healthy	prompt	supportive	respectful
self-disciplined	good	good cook	risk-taker
sincere	good taste	good listener	skillful
successful	leader	compassionate	good citizen
idealistic	competitive	spontaneous	tolerant
gracious	good sense of humor	good at ____	fun-loving
disciplined	mature	upbeat	loyal
accomplished	athletic	wise	generous
outspoken	ethical	flexible	empathetic

CHOOSE YOUR NEGATIVE CHARACTERISTICS FROM THE FOLLOWING LIST. CIRCLE THOSE ADJECTIVES THAT ARE APPLICABLE TO YOU MOST OF THE TIME

angry	jealous	hostile	worrying
unkind	petulant	insensitive	arrogant
mean	anxious	dishonest	greedy
surly	blames others	paranoid	manipulative
pessimistic	depressed	impatient	lazy
irritable	boring	irresponsible	rude
sarcastic	passive	gossipy	sexist
shallow	unethical	bossy	promiscuous
prejudiced	unreliable	cold	intolerant
obsessive	humorless	righteous	unreliable
ruthless	vengeful	frustrated	fearful
disrespectful	disloyal	childish	braggart
disorganized	spineless	hysterical	cowardly
bigoted	dirty	joyless	nervous

Was your "recognition" list longer for your positive characteristics than your "recall" list? Was the difference between the number of positive characteristics and negative characteristics substantial? Do you have a tendency to give yourself less credit than is constructive? Keep your list of positive characteristics handy. We will be using them again shortly.

If you accept the goal of improving upon your self-esteem, let me suggest a simple, but useful assignment. Make a contract with yourself that you will recite five positive characteristics before you engage in some particular behavior of your choosing. This practice is called "Grandma's Law." It works on the principle that we can increase the occurrence of a low probability behavior (like a child eating peas) if we make a high probability behavior (eating ice cream) contingent upon it. In other words, by making a contract that the children must eat their peas before they get their dessert, we increase the frequency of eating the peas. I recommend to you that you increase the frequency of your recollection of your positive characteristics. Do this by not allowing yourself to engage in a high frequency behavior (washing your hands) unless you first recite your list of positive characteristics.

From the list on page 172 of high frequency behaviors such as going to the refrigerator, etc., make a contract such as "Before I open the refrigerator for the next two weeks, I will first recite to myself five positive characteristics."

Such a contract may feel silly to some and is certainly mechanical in nature. It does have a robotic sense to it but, for those individuals who are insensitive to their positive characteristics, behaviors and values, it serves a very useful purpose.

At a time in my life when I had strong feelings of inadequacies, I followed my own prescription. It was instrumental in reversing a style of thinking that had little merit. So much so that several years ago, and many years after my utilization of "Grandma's Law," I was attending a workshop during which the workshop leader requested that we write down our positive characteristics. Within a few minutes I was able to list thirty-five. I rush to assure you that my ability to list a plethora of positive remarks does not diminish my awareness of my deficiencies. Nor does such a recognition of capabilities necessarily lead to a state of arrogance. Instead, I believe I have a fuller awareness of who I am, bright spots and blemishes, and a greater ability to cope with the struggles of life.

THE PRACTICE OF "GRANDMA'S LAW":

INCREASING AWARENESS OF POSITIVE

CHARACTERISTICS AND VALUES

Step 1:Establish a list of your positive characteristics.

Step 2:Choose two behaviors (from the list below or from your own mental review) that are frequent in your daily life.

chew gum	drink soft drinks
drink coffee	make a telephone call
go to the refrigerator	watch the news on TV
change your clothes	water your plants
pet your cat/dog	read the newspaper
read a book	drive your car

Step 3:Using the examples below, make a "Grandma's Law" contract with yourself to increase the frequency that you bring your positive characteristics and values into your awareness.

Example:

> For the next two weeks, I will remind myself of five positive characteristics or values before allowing myself to engage in any two of the most frequent behaviors I have chosen from the above list.

Example:
> I promise to tell myself that I am kind, gener-
> ous, sensitive, caring and a bright person be-
> fore I allow myself to drink a pop or have a cup
> of coffee for the next two weeks starting today
> (date _____).

My contract:
> I promise

_____

_____

_____

_____

_____

A major test of good self-esteem is the handling of criticism—real, implied or imagined. People with poor self-esteem are especially concerned with the possibility of being
berated and go to great lengths to avoid it. This behavior is
often the result of an "imprinting" of a traumatic childhood
experience or a generous portion of criticism from a fault
finding authority figure. The resulting behavior can be pas-
sivity, excessive pleasing, shyness, isolation or other action
generated to avoid the possibility of being criticized or hu-
miliated.

Interestingly, the same person with poor self-esteem will
often be unaware that their actions are based on self-
deprecating thoughts. When life has been filled by literally
thousands of such thoughts, perceptions become reduced
to feelings. Such people may only know that a situation is
uncomfortable but be unaware that similar situations have
been filled with self-deprecating thoughts and
misperceptions. Now in the situation once again, the
complete thought may be hidden, just a truncated version of

the original. Psychologists often uncover these feeling and their concomitant thoughts with a bit of probing:

> Psychologist: I understand that you had a miserable time at the party.
>
> Patient: I hate parties.
>
> Psychologist: What's so bad about parties?
>
> Patient: They're so boring and superficial. People just trying to play power games. Trying to impress everyone.
>
> Psychologist: And you don't like power games?
>
> Patient: No, my parents liked power games. I don't. They always made a big deal of their education, their titles, their accomplishments, always criticizing me for not living up to my potential.

For this man the avalanche of criticism he received as a child does not come into his everyday perception. All he knows is that he is uncomfortable in most social gatherings. In reality he is afraid of not living up to artificial standards and experiences. He is not aware of the whole thought process, just of a knot in his stomach or a general malaise. The fear, based upon his poor self-esteem, is that once again he'll be measured and found wanting.

The distortions in this man's thinking are many. He is guilty of very selective thinking, mind reading, and overgeneralization. His strong fear of criticism makes him most vulnerable to it. And fear fuels his distortions. Most of all, this man, and virtually all individuals with poor self-esteem, has a poor *mental ecology* which is detrimental to his well-being. His mind is polluted with belittling remarks ("There you go again, screwing up"), disparaging comments ("I wish I had at least one talent. I know a little of many things but I'm not really good at anything"), and self-defeating overgeneralizations ("I'll never amount to anything").

In the context of an abundance of self-deprecating thoughts and an absence of positive awareness, any remark hinting at criticism becomes fully absorbed. The individual with a poor mental ecology is hypersensitive to further punishment (criticism) and is inadequately prepared for criticism. Unlike the cybernetics rocket discussed earlier, that takes negative information objectively and use it constructively, the poor self-esteem individual's antennae is hypersensitive to irrelevant static. When authentic criticism appears he overreacts to it.

Coupled with the pattern noted above is an inability to place criticism, real or imaginary, in perspective. In the extreme case, the individual with poor self-esteem fails to allow personal compassion for himself and a sense of a lifetime vision to come into view. Each event is considered another example of his own inadequacy. Filtered out of examination are those occasions of success, endurance, and achievement. Contrast the negative pattern noted for poor self-esteem with a very positive self-esteem and the use of negative information.

Edward O. Wilson,—Professor at Harvard University, winner of two Pulitzer prizes, and world renowned naturalist writes this of himself:

> *"I am blind in one eye and cannot hear high frequency sounds; therefore I am an entomologist. I cannot memorize lines, have trouble visualizing words spelled out to me letter by letter, and am often unable to get digits in the right order while reading and copying numbers. So I contrived ways of expressing ideas that others can recite with quotations and formulas. This compensation is aided by an unusual ability to make comparisons of disparate objects, thus to produce*

syntheses of previously unconnected information. I write smoothly, in part I believe because my memory is less encumbered by the phrasing and nuances of others. I pushed these strengths and skirted the weaknesses. " [55]

In the case of this extraordinary individual, an awareness of his deficits was matched by a sensitivity to his strengths. No undue emphasis was placed on his inadequacies. No sense of victimization was present, but instead a factual acceptance of characteristics that he had little ability to alter. Notice the ability to be kind to oneself, to be aware of strengths, to take pride in accomplishments and to be compassionate with circumstances.

The chapter on self-esteem has been filled with exercises: an exercise requesting that you recall those difficulties in your life that you have overcome or survived and an exercise which encourages you to create a "smile file" containing documents recalling positive experiences. You were asked to list your positive and negative characteristics and compare your recollections with lists that I generated. And you were asked to commit to a contract based upon "Grandma's law" for the purpose of increasing the frequency in which you bring your positive characteristics to mind. The exercises were created to help you process information constructively, help improve your mental ecology, increase your awareness of personal strengths and strengthen your sense of perspective. These exercises are not new to me. I have utilized them in my own life for many years and have recommended them to thousands of patients. I am confident that if you do the same, your self-esteem and your life will be better for the effort.

**I commit myself to take care of
myself for the sake of myself, my
family, my friends, my community
and my country**

4790-PAWL

Chapter 10

QUALITIES NECESSARY IN THE PURSUIT

OF WELL-BEING

CLARIFYING and enhancing your character is not a guarantee of well-being. Happiness and well-being come from a variety of factors, character being only one of the influences. However, while enhancing our own character, it is of interest to consider those qualities that are critical to happiness and well-being.

Dr. David G. Myers wrote a wonderful book entitled, *The Pursuit of Happiness: Discovering the pathway to fulfillment, well-being, and enduring personal joy.* As a social psychologist, Myers reviewed thousands of studies in search of the key to happiness and well-being. Some of his findings were surprising. Age, gender, race, location, education, even tragic disability, mattered little. The things that did matter:

". . . renewing sleep and periodic solitude; traits such as self-esteem, sense of personal control, optimism and extraversion; work and other activities that enhance our identity and absorb us into flow; close supportive friendships and marriages."[56]

Many of these factors are available to us if we choose to focus upon them as a priority. This list contains factors that are personal habits and attributes directly under our control (physical fitness, periodic solitude, optimism, extraversion, work and other activities which enhance identity) and areas that are somewhat more in the control of others (friendships and marriages). Each element has considerable merit, but it is worthwhile to attend to those most directly under our control and most associated with our understanding of character.

I believe that well-being, in itself, is a worthwhile overt goal and that we can increase our likelihood of experiencing well-being by mapping out a plan. Consider the following formula: A sense of well-being is most likely to occur in one who: a) focuses on positive experiences (that is, is optimistic) b) feels a sense of fulfillment and c) is in touch with the sensations of life MOST OF THE TIME.

PURSUING WELL-BEING

The first part of the formula is to **focus on positive experiences**—that is, to be optimistic. Probably the most well known expert on the topic of optimism is Martin Seligman.[57] Seligman, a psychologist, became well known for his investigations of depression and coining the term "learned helplessness." After spending decades investigating how a sense of helplessness can be learned and be central to depression, Seligman decided to examine the converse process—optimism. Optimism, like depression and learned helplessness, is not typically innate but rather a learned process. Seligman states that there are three specific patterns

of beliefs differentiating the pessimist and the optimist—
three thinking styles that cause the pessimist to feel helpless
and destroy virtually every aspect of his life. He calls these
three categories: **permanent, pervasive and personal.**

PERMANENT

People whose language is laced with "always" and "never"
tend to be pessimists. They are likely to see the difficulties in
their lives as permanent. These are the individuals whom
you may hear complaining that, "Bad things always happen
to me" and "I never win at anything." More than just a language style this pattern of perceiving life as black and white
and universally negative has a profound effect on the
individual's sense of well-being. While we all experience
the trials and tribulations of life, the pessimist allows the
hurt to be extrapolated into a more long-lasting event. Negatives are permanent in nature and positives fleeting or temporary. "This is my lucky day" but "Bad things are always happening to me" illustrates how the good events become framed
in a temporary or happenstance picture while the negatives
have a never-ending nature.

Listen to the language of someone you consider pessi-
mistic. Notice the frequent occurrence of statements that
connote a sense of hopelessness—a sense that the world is
permanently tainted and there is nothing to be done about
it (but perhaps complain).

By contrast, the optimist's language is peppered with
words like "sometimes," words that reflect an understanding
that life has "grays." The optimist views situations as change-
able, especially when they are negative. "This too will pass" is
an underlying theme of the optimists. The optimist is more
prone to perceive that negative events are time limited. He
believes that for every difficulty there is something positive

to look forward to. A person with such an interpretative style is comfortable with the notion that feelings represent a temporary state.

The optimist is the exact opposite of the pessimist. Where the pessimist sees the negative as permanent, the optimist sees a temporary state. Where the pessimist views positive events as temporary, the optimist views them as the norm.

A practical means of maintaining an optimistic outlook is to keep many of the exercises implemented in this book easily accessible. For example, tendencies toward pessimism and feeling of the permanence of difficulties can be offset by referring to the exercise, "Things I Have Overcome and Survived", in Chapter 9. This exercise provides direct evidence that the stresses in your life are not permanent. You have survived numerous challenges and undoubtedly will survive more. Reminding yourself of the specific battles you have won or survived can help provide the perspective needed to challenge distortions that your current trouble is overwhelming or permanent.

PERVASIVE

According to Seligman, the pessimist also has a strong tendency to view negative experiences as pervasive—to generalize from one event to a whole category or a universe of events. "Not only am I a failure in this one task but I can't do anything" is a good illustration of a pessimist's pervasive outlook. Notice how self-defeating this thinking can be. By expanding one difficulty, fear, or failure into an entire range of events, the pessimist defeats himself before he even gets started. His tendency to predict disaster before he acts, in effect, paralyzes him and limits his creativity.

Notice too, the effects perceiving negatives as universal have on feelings of hopefulness. Hopefulness is the fulcrum of optimism. It stands as the heart and the base of the optimist's process of handling life's barriers. By limiting the trials of life to the event itself and maintaining a hope that something better is right around the corner, the optimist moves forward meeting each day as a new event. The pessimist, on the other hand, undermines any feelings of hopefulness by generalizing from one event and thereby destroying the sense of promise. When hope is gone, despair cannot be far behind.

The tendency toward perceiving negative events as pervasive, too, can be combated by the use of exercises in this book. In particular, the "Smile File" exercise in Chapter 9 reminds you that others consider you a worthwhile person with admirable traits. While you may not have done as well as you might like in one instance, there are a multitude of other occasions in which you exhibited praiseworthy behaviors. If you have a tendency to believe that you're always doing the wrong thing and never the right, then keeping a copy of your "Smile File" handy might be a useful strategy to reduce this pattern. Examining your Smile File might also remind you to call that friend whose remark, letter, or card was important enough to place in your file. They might have a different perspective on your current problem—one that says your behavior is not so pervasive as you might think.

PERSONALIZATION

The third leg of Seligman's differentiation between optimism and pessimism is personalization. For the pessimist, personalization refers to the tendency to see problems as personal defects (e.g., "I'm stupid"). At the same time, anything positive in the pessimist's life is seen as unrelated to his personal effort or ability. Optimists, on the other hand, take credit for good things happening to them and tend to blame circumstances for the negatives in their life (e.g., "I grew up in a rough environment"). This difference in the way the pessimist and optimist "personalize" is critical to how each feels about himself and his personal sense of control. If I am a pessimist, I am prone to feel inadequate. Negative events that happen to me are my responsibility. If I am an optimist, I am more likely to feel that the negative events are external to me and that I can problem-solve to change such events. I feel in greater control.

How we personalize is fundamental to our self-esteem and to how we manage our stress, and our emotions. In each circumstance the manner in which we interpret experiences is the governing mechanism for controlling emotions and feelings. This is especially true as it pertains to responding to failures. Seligman argues:

> *"What is crucial is what you think when you fail, using the power of 'non-negative thinking.' Changing the destructive things you say to yourself when you experience the setbacks that life deals all of us is the central skill of optimism."* [58]

Once again, referring to the exercise "Things I have Overcome or Survived" can be a useful strategy. Reminding yourself that you have overcome many challenges in your life is valuable when meeting a new challenge.

"Choosing a Positive Model" in Chapter 6 might also be useful. A critical question to ask yourself is whether the person you admire and have chosen as a positive model has gone through challenging times. If you have investigated that person's life in some depth, it is highly likely that his or her life has involved some periods of significant stress, failure and self-doubt. If this person's successes are valuable enough to remember, so are his or her difficult periods.

PESSIMISM, OPTIMISM AND HEALTH

Optimism is a wonderful quality to have as one element in the make-up of character. There is another very practical reason for pursuing optimism—the benefit such a style has for your health. Seligman comments on the relationship between optimism and health as follows:

> "Consider a pessimistic person who believes that sickness is permanent, pervasive, and personal. 'Nothing I do matters,' he believes, 'so why do anything?' Such a person is less likely to give up smoking, get flu shots, diet, exercise, go to the doctor when ill, or even follow medical advice."

Referring to a thirty-five year long study of one hundred Harvard graduates conducted by George Vaillant, Seligman says:

> "...Pessimists were in fact found to be less likely than optimists to give up cigarettes, and more likely to suffer illness. So optimists, who readily take matters into their own hands, are more likely to take action that prevents illness or get it treated once illness strikes."[59]

WE ALL (BOTH PESSIMISTS AND

OPTIMISTS) CHOOSE OUR "DATA"

Seligman points out that our explanatory style of life is probably learned at an early age but is subject to modification. At the heart of Seligman's research and analysis is the assumption that what is crucial to a happy and successful life is what we say to ourselves as we experience the inevitable pitfalls and failures of life. Also crucial to any attempt at modification is an understanding that we "choose our data."

Some Americans truly believe that the 1990s represented a disastrous state of affairs and can provide data to prove it. To illustrate how happiness and optimism are relative, take the following historical tour. Examine each decade of the twentieth century and ask yourself if you would like to trade the 1990's for any of these periods.

Highlights of the Ten Decades in the Twentieth Century

1900 - 1910	The first decade of the new century began with the assassination of President William McKinley on Sept. 2, 1901. Death during this period from epidemics of influenza and pneumonia was frequent as was the scourge of tuberculosis and gastroenteritis.
1911 - 1920	This was a period of significant growth coupled with the U.S. participation in World War I. The country suffered over 317,000 casualties in the war. [60]
1921 - 1930	A decade in which there was massive lynching of blacks in the South and the rise of the Klu Klux Klan. The end of the decade was punctuated by the fall of the stock market.
1931 - 1940	The 1930s are remembered as the heart of the "Great Depression" with massive amounts of unemployment, foreclosures and suicides.
1940 - 1949	This decade is most strongly represented by the United States involvement in World War II. Americans paid for their victory with 1,058,000 casualties and 248,000 killed. [61]
1950 - 1959	The early years of this decade show the nation involved in another multinational conflict (the Korean war), coupled with the McCarthy era and beginnings of a national obsession with Communism.

1960-1969	The 1960s was a decade of conflict accentuated by the assassination of three national leaders (John F. Kennedy, Martin Luther King and Robert Kennedy). Tremendous friction existed between American citizens over the morality of the Vietnamese War.
1970-1979	The first portion of this decade continued the national debate concerning the Vietnam conflict, now expanded into Cambodia. Shortly thereafter the Watergate burglary occurred, precipitating a constitution crisis and the resignation of the President. The latter portion of this decade saw a long line at America's gas pumps and a long siege as the country weathered the holding of American hostages by Iranian militants.
1980-1989	One-hundred and sixty-one American Marines were killed in a terrorist attack at a Beirut, Lebanon bombing. U.S. Forces invaded Grenada; corporate takeovers escalated, widely contributing to very significant disparity between economic classes in the United States.
1990-1999	"Desert Storm," a limited war between the United States and Iraq, began the early part of the decade. Subsequently the United States public was consumed by the murder trial of celebrity O.J. Simpson, the sexual misconduct of President Bill Clinton and Congress's unsuccessful attempt to impeach him.

Undoubtedly others could draw a much different historical perspective than the one I have chosen. One could easily highlight positive events—discoveries, inventions, medical progress, etc. The point is that we choose our data and it is easy to get caught up in current stresses and lose the broader perspective. When the current decade is examined in contrast to periods of the twentieth century, it takes on an entirely different perspective.

How we experience our life is a function of how we perceive our experiences. Our experiences are not the only reality, they are our perceptions. This point is clearly illustrated by one of my favorite authors, Robert Fulghum. Fulghum, a Unitarian minister, is well known for his book *All I Ever Needed To Know I Learned In Kindergarten*. He is a wonderful teller of insightful stories and, in one such story, tells of a summer experience he had as a young man working at a western resort.[62] The distinctive characteristic of this work experience for Fulghum was not the hard work but the food—the sameness of the food.

> *"One week the employees had been served the same thing for lunch every single day. Two wieners, a mound of sauerkraut, and stale rolls. To compound insult with injury, the cost of meals was deducted from our check."*

He describes one particular night when he was "pitching a fit" over the food when he was joined by a night auditor named Sigmund Wollman.

> *"Put a bloodhound in a suit and tie and you have Sigmund Wollman. He's got good reason to look sorrowful. Survivor of Auschwitz. Three years. German Jew. Thin, coughed a lot. He liked being alone at the night job—gave him intellectual space, gave him peace and quiet, and even more, he could go into the kitchen and have a snack whenever he wanted—all the wieners and sauerkraut he wanted."*

Now Fulghum and Wollman's shift overlapped by one hour and Wollman came upon Fulghum on the night he was "pitching his fit":

'Fulchum, are you finished?'

'No. Why?'

'Lissen, Fulchum. Lissen me, lissen. You know what's
wrong with you? It's not wieners and kraut and it's
not the boss and it's not the chef and it's not this job.'

'So what's wrong with me?'

'Fulchum, you think you know everything, but you
don't know the difference between an inconvenience
and a problem. If you break you neck, if you have
nothing to eat, if your house is on fire—then you got
a problem. Everything else is inconvenience. Life is
inconvenient. Life is lumpy. Learn to separate the
inconvenience from the real problems. You will live
longer. And will not annoy people like me so much.
Good night.'

In a gesture combining dismissal and blessing he waved
me off to bed."

Know the difference between an inconvenience and a problem—quite an important lesson. The optimist appears to
understand the lesson—knowing the difference between
an inconvenience and a problem.

FEELING A SENSE OF FULFILLMENT AND

MISSION

Optimism is the first trait I recommend for your consid-
eration. The second dimension of my definition of well-being is **feeling a sense of fulfillment**. In recent years I have
conducted a series of lectures and discussions in two state
prisons. Walking into a maximum-security prison is an incredible experience. Your television images are probably

somewhat accurate—the harsh, cold, dehumanizing environment and the small cells are there before your eyes. What you cannot fully sense on your television set is the daily fear, the lack of privacy, the constant noise, the loneliness and the danger. I do not speak as an expert. I speak as a visitor to two state prisons for a total of perhaps 30 hours. I simply share with you that men in this stressful environment vary widely in their ability to cope. The most remarkable point, however, is that some are happy—happier than any other time in their life. I have repeatedly asked my prison audiences "Is it possible to be happy in prison?" I have never heard any prisoner say no.

When I share this information with other audiences, surprise is the most common reaction. The loss of freedom in the austere dangerous prison environment, void of the people and things we love, seems a hardship unbearable to manage. And yet this most harsh existence is, for some, a place where satisfaction is found.

There are other examples even more amazing: the extreme case of Viktor Frankl, the Jewish psychiatrist imprisoned in the Nazi concentration camps of War World II. Gordon Allport describes Frankl's experience as follows:

> *"As a longtime prisoner in bestial concentration camps he found himself stripped to naked existence. His father, mother, brother, and his wife died in camps or were sent to the gas ovens, so that, except for his sister, his entire family perished in these camps. How could he—every possession lost, every value destroyed, suffering from hunger, cold and brutality, hourly expecting extermination—how could he find life worth preserving?"* [63]

What Frankl found, in a setting where the probability of survival was remote, was an unlikely insight. He found, at that critical moment when overwhelmed by the immensity of the horror surrounding and engulfing him, the meaning to go forward. He decided his purpose—his reason for being. It was to tell the scientific community and beyond the psychology of the concentration camps. He imagined himself lecturing to audiences, describing the dynamic of survival. Frankl spent three years in hard labor, amid starvation and almost daily beating. He observed cruelty beyond description but still was able to write:

> *"We who lived in concentration camps can remember the men who walked through the huts comforting others, giving away their last piece of bread. They may have been few in number, but they offer sufficient proof that everything can be taken from man but one thing: the last of human freedom—to choose one's attitude in any given set of circumstances, to choose one's way."* [64]

He goes on to say:

> *"Woe to him who saw no more sense in his life, no aim, no purpose, and therefore no point in carrying on. He was soon lost."* [65]

Examples like those of concentration camps are so dramatic that we can easily forget the principle behind the observation—the key to survival lies in our power to discover meaning in our life. This personal insight can relate to more than just surviving, however. It can be a key to our well-being.

Returning to my visits to the State prisons for a moment, the first time I asked my audience whether it was possible to be happy in prison I received the strongest reply from a 29-year-old serving a life sentence for murder. His meaning in life was not spiritual or charitable but quite self-centered. He spoke with great pride of his belief that he was the best basketball guard in the entire prison. Now, others can be angry at the injustice of this young man finding satisfaction when much of society would like for him to live a life of suffering commensurate with the magnitude of his crime. Putting the issue of justice aside, however, we can immediately be struck by each person's ability to find that something in his life in which he can find meaning. The individuality of pain, suffering, pleasure and happiness are governed not by external forces but by internal decisions, beliefs and attitudes. Mahatma Gandhi stated it thus:

> *"Happiness does not come with things, even 20th century things. It can come from work and pride in what you do."*

Discovering one's purpose can take many forms, some majestic, some simple. Each, however, can have its own beauty. A favorite story is one told by a patient about his father, a car mechanic. The son proudly told me that his father was a mechanical genius who could fix almost anything. Although his mechanical skills were legendary in his rural setting, the father went one step further. It was the father's practice not to charge anyone who couldn't afford payment. His father's philosophy was, "If you pay me, you'll never remember what I did. But if I fix your car for free, you'll never forget me." This man certainly had a purpose and just as certainly was leaving a legacy.

If we are to systematically pursue the goal of well-being, we should clarify what purpose we have in life. We should also make sure that some portion of each day is set aside for the primary purpose we find in life.

A practical means of making the above goal realistic is to keep your personal eulogy and mission statement handy. These two exercises get at those goals you consider the most sacred. Why not have statements that focus on your highest priority in a place where they can remind you to stay on track?

Why live a life consumed by those activities you consider less than critical? And remember, a small amount of time devoted each day to goals you value will reduce the stress associated with other necessary but less desirable activities. Keeping your mission and eulogy exercises in a visible place will also be an apt reminder to take care of yourself first for the benefit of yourself and those around you.

BEING IN TOUCH WITH THE

SENSATIONS OF LIFE

Well-being involves **being in touch with the sensations of life**. It is an interesting to note where "troubled" people spend most of their time mentally. It certainly is not in the present. Those who are predominately depressed, sour, or frequently frustrated tend to focus on the past, while those who are anxious, fearful or worried are concerned about the future. Both are destroying the present. Leo Buscaglia, the late author and motivational speaker, told a story with Buddhist origins which addresses this issue. I call it the "berry story":

> *"A young man is walking by the edge of a jungle, only to realize that a ferocious tiger has just emerged and is stalking him. Terrified, he turns and runs as fast as he can with the tiger in immediate pursuit. He quickly reaches a cliff where he must make a decision in how he will die, for the tiger is but a few feet away and the cliff is at least a thousand feet high. He chooses to jump but immediately upon his fall grabs onto a berry bush over the edge of the cliff. As the branch begins to break, he reaches over and picks a berry."* [66]

Those hearing or reading the story for the first time are often somewhat confused because the story does not have a clear ending. But, of course, the story is really a parable. The lesson is that the man had only a moment to live and chose to live that moment in the most valuable way—to make the most of what was available at the time. To live neither in the past nor the future.

The parable teaches a lesson often learned by those whose lives have been threatened. Victims of cancer, heart attacks and other life-threatening events often reappraise their priorities and relationships and reorder their values. UCLA psychologists Shelley Taylor and Rebecca Collins, after interviewing dozens of women diagnosed with breast cancer, were surprised to discover that many felt they benefited from their experience. [67] Their diagnoses afforded the opportunity to focus on each moment, hour, day. It is common to anticipate the pleasure of the next vacation, the next raise, the next promotion—only to miss out on the wonders of our daily lifes. When the potential of those daily experiences is lost, we regret our failure to enjoy the moments of our life. In the words of Wayne Dyer, *"The highest form of sanity is living in the present moment."* [68]

Becoming sensitive to the value of each moment in life is illustrated in an amusing way by a popular comic who does a routine on being "next." He tells of the delight in being next in line at the bank, at the movies and other places where he is excited about being the next to be served. He revels in this experience so much that when it's his turn, he lets others get in front of him so he can extend the enjoyment of being "next."

Being in touch with the sensations of life is also the essence of what psychologist Jon Kabit-Zenn calls mindfulness. [69] In such wonderful books as *Full Catastrophe Living* and *Wherever You Go There You Are*, Kabit-Zenn describes a form of meditation that centers on the experience at hand, cultivating the awareness of life's sensations.

While I recommend the practice of meditation, and in particular mindfulness, I suggest that the even more fundamental practice of taking five minutes each day to center yourself and focus on your existence. In the beautifully written parable, *The One Minute Manager,* Ken Blanchard & Spencer Johnson[70] commend the benefits of taking a few minutes each day to set aside the responsibilities of the day and to focus on those things that are truly meaningful for you. Whether setting aside time to meditate or just centering on deeper values of life, focusing on the moment is a major means of increasing well-being.

In our achievement and action oriented society, doing nothing is viewed with disdain. Associated with laziness and sloth, inactivity is perceived to be wasteful. Such a viewpoint confuses activity with meaningfullness—a point readily disputed when we consider the merit of many activities performed in the course of the day. Another, more thoughtful, perspective might be to evaluate the moments of our life from the perspective of whether we felt as if we really lived them—experienced them in depth and felt alive from the experience. Such feelings would not be limited to pleasure but would include the full range of emotions, as well as quiet and contemplation. Such a perception adds meaning to life—a fullness absent from the experiences of all too many people in the bustle of modern society.

Too often the tendency to focus on difficulties of the past or worries concerning the future stem from measuring your actions by external measures such as status, power, wealth, and the judgment of others. Challenge these tendencies by referring back to your "Code of Conduct and Values"—the standards personally created by you. Separate yourself from external control, allow yourself to gain control of your own feelings and work to stay in the moment as much as possible.

"MOST OF THE TIME"

Happiness is a contrast state. It is necessary to have felt some degree of unhappiness in order to appreciate the experience of well-being. Will Carleton noted:

> *"To appreciate heaven well, 'tis good for a man to have some fifteen minutes of hell."*[71]

Well-being is also not a permanent state achieved for eternity. Winston Churchill said, "Success is never final." Neither is happiness. Dr. Ed Diener, writing of his investigations of people who evaluate their lives as positives, states:

> *"It appears that the life with an occasional intense positive experience, but with a moderate level of pleasant emotional experience most of the time, is likely to lead an individual to evaluate his or her life in a positive way."*[72]

Learning to appreciate and increase the small pleasures of life, while simultaneously working to manage and accept the negatives, will accomplish much more than awaiting that supreme moment of ecstasy.

Individual character has many different qualities. Some of these qualities appear to be particularly useful in the pursuit of well-being and the three suggested here—optimism, a sense of purpose and a focus upon the present—are well worth pursuing.

In this pursuit, I recommend reviewing some of the earlier exercises and keeping them close at hand:

- To help to maintain an optimistic viewpoint: "Things I Have Overcome" and "Choosing a Positive Model."
- To help to maintain your sense of purpose: "Writing Your Mission Statement" and "Your Eulogy."
- To help to maintain a focus on the moment as a primary goal: "Code of Conduct and Values."

The above efforts may not be where you wish to place your energy. The choice is yours. Well-being is not luck, happenstance or good fortune. It takes effort and undoubtedly is more likely to occur in those individuals who develop qualities such as optimism and cultivating a sense of purpose and setting aside time to focus on those things that are truly meaningful.

I commit myself to take care of myself for the sake of myself, my family, my friends, my community and my country

Chapter 11

REFLECTIONS

BOOKS are always a reflection of their authors. This book is no
different. It mirrors my struggles, feelings and thoughts about
my career and personal experiences. If I may, I would like to
briefly describe some early childhood difficulties, my battle to
overcome them and how I came to believe so fervently in the
importance of rehabilitation and character. Before I begin, I
want to tell you with all due modesty that I have been a university professor for 30 years, attaining the rank of full professor at
the unusually young age of 41. Additionally, I give 20 to 40
speeches annually and have numerous requests for my presentation and workshops. It was not always so.

I stuttered extremely badly as a child. For as long as I can
remember, I struggled with my speech and consequently
with my interactions with others. My speech impediment was
severe enough that I had major secondary characteristics.
Most of us are acquainted with these in the form of intense
facial grimaces, distortions, and long tension filled periods

in which my breath was "caught" and every throat and facial muscle tensed. The listener too was tied up in this pressure, often showing his anxiety, and frequently filling in the word before I could say it (a very embarrassing and discounting thing for the stutterer).

This is a classic picture of a severe stutterer and most people have at least seen it, if not been a part of the relationship. Such a dysfunction has a defining influence upon an individual's personality, self–esteem and view of life. That was certainly the case in my life. Like any severe stutterer, I would awaken each morning, projecting my fears onto the day by analyzing with whom I was going to speak, how I could avoid making a fool of myself, and recalling my past failures. My classroom experiences were often occasions of terror and my interactions with "friends" a series of taunts and ridicule.

I remember one particularly painful experience in eighth grade Latin class, a subject in which I had no proficiency and probably would have feared even without my impediment. On this particular day, my efforts at hiding behind the student in front of me were unsuccessful and I was called upon to conjugate a verb in Latin. Initially I hardly made a sound but, to my dismay, the teacher did not call upon another student and expected me to persist. After much mental gymnastics, I settled on the first word in this conjugation, which began with the letter "q." Only my mouth did not follow the directions of my mind. Quite the contrary. I began to build up a level of air tension of the highest intensity and with it the suspense and the tension of my fellow students. When the sound finally erupted, after what may actually have been two minutes, it came rushing in the loud, forced words, "quack, quack." The class exploded in a pandemonium of laughter. In spite of the teacher's best efforts, it took her a good deal of time to regain her composure and the class's attention. I put on my best face, but felt the depths of embarrassment and despair.

In my mind, these "acute" episodes were surrounded by the daily misery of attempting to cope with a behavior (stuttering) which defined who I was. I certainly believed that anyone wishing to know me would be told by others that "he was the kid that stutters." Many childhood experiences of stuttering are exactly that, childhood experiences which do not persist into adulthood. I was not so fortunate. My stutter persevered through adolescence into my adult years. During adolescence, I did not date and put my energies into sports, where I could obtain some small measure of achievement. Since I was almost the smallest boy in my school, these attempts too were only moderately successful.

My college years were also substantially influenced by my stutter and it's accompanying poor self–esteem. My stutter at this point in my life was not as obvious and frequent as it had been as a child. I was more capable of selecting my words and more able to control the situations in which I would be placed. Through a series of fortuitous circumstances, I actually ended up in a teaching position, following the work for my master's degree, at the University Of Winnipeg, in Manitoba, Canada.

I had found that I could control my speech impediment to a large degree by two procedures. If I read my lecture notes and did not look at the students and, secondly, if I assiduously avoided words that began with troublesome sounds, I could make it through a class. Being read to by a teacher who avoids eye contact and struggles through his material, however, does not make for a very outstanding classroom experience. The feedback from my poor performance immediately escalated my already high feelings of anxiety. As these feelings grew they were accompanied by depression and even poorer performance. At the same time, I began to avoid the terrible experience of nervousness and sweating during each class by canceling my classes with frequency. This, of course, ended me up in my chairman's office who, although very kind, stated that such behavior was not permissible. I had to either teach all my classes or leave. I remember this as one of the lowest points in my life. I felt that I was incapable of reversing an intractable dysfunction. I was dejected and depressed.

At this point, I asked a friend for advice. He recommended that I see a psychologist that he knew, not for my stutter, but for my depression. Since I believed my options were limited, I reluctantly followed his recommendation. My first appointment at the psychologist's office was quite a surprise even though I had been teaching undergraduate classes on the subject. This pleasant man kept asking me who I was and I, in turn, repeatedly stuttered my way through my name. Not to be deterred, he gently but persistently asked that I tell him about my characteristics–that is, who I was. And I just as persistently told him (in my very belabored fashion) that I was there to have him help me overcome my stutter. At last, I understood that if I was going to proceed with this man, I was going to have to tell him who I was, my characteristics, me. I was going to have to be more than just my stutter (my symptoms).

This excellent psychologist[73] looked at my problem from an entirely different perspective than the numerous speech therapists who I had seen throughout my life. He, too, saw that the speech impediment was having a profound effect upon me, but viewed the problem as much more all encompassing. My now firmly entrenched poor self–esteem and constant anxiety were major contributing factors. My avoidance of words and situations perpetuated my very intense stutter. It was not simply my stutter that needed to be treated, it was my thinking style, my poor coping skills and the quality of my life.

The actual treatment over the course of weekly visits for a year followed logically from this new perspective. The issue was no longer simply the speech impediment, but my lack of awareness of my admirable qualities and how the stutter interacted with loss of self–esteem, my feelings of depression and avoidance behaviors. Since these patterns encouraged the primary symptom of stuttering, a new approach was appropriate. The focus was not directed toward the stutter as the primary cause of the poor self–esteem and depression (although obviously it was a factor). That approach had already been tried and was found to be ineffective. The focus was on who I was—surely I had characteristics other than the one negative behavior I so tenaciously and myopically saw. Surely I had other qualities and values. Gradually my therapist and I dug them up and polished them off. Slowly I began to define my character.

Just as importantly, I began to understand that blaming all the suffering in my life on my stutter was *destructive*. Instead, I was taught the means by which I could build up my self–esteem and reduce the feelings of depression. There was still, however, the matter of the stutter. Here too, the problem was put in a different perspective. It was no longer just a contraction or spasm of the vocal cords, but now a set of avoidant behaviors and self–destructive thoughts. ("I will only be a worthwhile person if I can always speak fluently," "It's better not to speak and make a fool of myself than to try to speak.") With a new definition of the problem came another means of approaching the problem. Each and every day, I was required to talk, talk, talk. I was required to frequently use the telephone (a most feared activity for anyone with a severe stutter), introduce myself, and ask questions of store clerks, policemen, and strangers. I had to work daily on changing the thought process before and after each speaking occasion. I had to learn to put my problem in perspective and drop my intense focus on just one goal—eliminating the speech impediment.

Interestingly, the amelioration of a problem (or an injury or a disease) is not always a straight line. In the course of the year, my speech impediment did reduce in frequency, but more important to me, I gained a greater sense of who I was and greater control over my life.

This is not a happily ever after story. Life is not a fairy tale. I did not speak fluently after one year nor did I always have a high sense of self–confidence and self–worth. My thoughts were not always constructive to my well–being nor nurturing to fluent speech. When I discontinued my treatment, however, I did have a strategy on how to manage my problem and enhance my health. This strategy was based on a premise which I have carried with me ever since. It is the belief that "The price of freedom is eternal vigilance." This statement, which I understand was first uttered by Thomas Jefferson referring to the need for the country to be on guard against potential aggression, was used to illustrate that chronic issues need daily attention.

The "eternal vigilance" concept hit me very hard just a few years ago when I attended the annual meeting of the American Pain Society. I attended this meeting often and always made an attempt to reestablish old acquaintances and friendships. Many of the people whom I saw at this meeting I had known for a long time. Some knew that I have wrestled with a speech impediment but most probably did not notice a small stutter in an otherwise normal communication. Not on this occasion. For reasons that I do not completely understand, my speech impediment returned and returned with full force. I found myself in the presence of well-known people in my field unable to speak without major contortions. My immediate reaction was one of surprise and embarrassment and then withdrawal. I withdrew to my hotel room and began a major blue funk. Fortunately, however, I came to my senses quickly. I realized that, whatever was the initiating cause of my stutter, I needed to take care of myself as a person in the full sense of the word and not concentrate upon the stutter. With considerable anxiety, I returned to full participation in the meeting, even seeking out the most prestigious of my colleagues. I worked on keeping my problem in perspective and concentrated on my own sense of who I was. I focused on my value as a person, not on avoiding, self-degrading, and worrying. "The price of freedom is eternal vigilance"—vigilance to practicing constructive behavior before, during, and after a crisis situation. My fluency was back within two days.

Since my initial therapy, I have attempted to use the recommendation that I give daily attention to my character, my self–esteem, my self–worth and my thought processes. I try never to avoid any interaction because of the potential of stuttering.[74] This doesn't mean that I haven't looked for ways to improve my speech. It does mean that I'm committed to looking at my character. It does mean that I am in control and managing my life.

I was fortunate to meet an excellent therapist. But I have learned both as a patient and as a therapist myself that the more the patient "brings to the table" in the form of character, the greater the likelihood of success. I have also learned that the solution or improvement of most chronic problems is not a straight line. I had spent many years seeing multiple speech therapists, seeking relief. For many young people these interventions worked. I was not in the favored group. What I have learned from this experience is that when problems become chronic, one may have to take an alternative route—one that does not seem to intuitively make sense.

The point is illustrated in my work with the chronic pain patient. Virtually all the chronic pain patients I have seen in my career are experiencing pain, suffering, and major alterations in their lifestyle. The most obvious solution to such a pattern is to relieve the pain, which would in turn reduce the suffering and allow the person to return to their previous lifestyle. Sounds reasonable. Only one major glitch, the patient is dealing with chronic pain. That first word, chronic means, by definition, that traditional medical methods have been ineffective in resolving the problem. Of course the patient can continue to seek additional physicians as I sought additional therapists. But, at some point, such an effort becomes not only non-productive but dangerous. The danger is both physical and mental. Physically, well-meaning physicians, accustomed to bodies that heal and trained to manage acute pain (not chronic), may prescribe inappropriate medications or surgeries. After a while, when this treatment is ineffective, they may suggest that the patient must just accept the suffering. The danger, mentally, is that the patient may believe them. Or the patient may allow their entire life to be consumed by the chronic pain. Such a response is understandable for pain is incredibly powerful. It's ability to dominate is legend.

If only we could relieve the pain, all the other misery would disappear. Here is where the seemingly illogical approach appears. When focusing on pain has been unsuccessful, the focus needs to turn to controlling the suffering and the "pain behaviors." Not an easy task. But control of suffering *is* within the patient's power, although control of the pain may not be.

There is wisdom in actively focusing on those things that you can control. You'll remember the same insight expressed in the serenity prayer:

> *"God grant me the serenity to accept things I cannot change, courage to change things I can, and wisdom to know the difference."*

When a problem become chronic, it can also become powerful, dominating a person's life. I certainly allowed my stutter to govern mine. But we need not limit this theme to speech dysfunctions and chronic pain. Actually pain comes in many forms—stressful jobs, marriages, relationships, financial concerns. All of these areas have the ability to suck the energy out of our lives if we allow it. This is our major failing—we allow it. We make the choice to continue to focus on the external stress instead of focusing on the internal person. We focus on the pain instead of controlling the suffering. We blame the stress or pain for the misery and thereby give it power.

I am reminded of a common exercise told to illustrate how difficult it is to change your focus. You may have heard it. Imagine a large, pink elephant. Now make sure you visualize all the details, his trunk, big powerful legs, his scrawny tail. Everything you can think of. Take your time to get him clearly visualized. Got it? Good.

Now, wipe clean any remote thought of that elephant for the next five seconds. Don't think any thoughts related to that elephant. One. . Two. . .Three. . .Four. . .Five. For most people erasing all thoughts of the elephant is very difficult and they laughingly admit so. But let's go on to the second part of this little game. This time visualize the most expensive car that you could possible buy. Pick your color, your upholstery, focus on the styling and the shining gleam of this brilliant new car. Got it? Really clear? Good.

During the exercise of visualizing the new car, did you think of a large, pink elephant? No, just as I thought.

The point of this little mental lesson is that the more direct energy we put into forgetting, the harder it becomes. (You may have experienced something similar when concentrating on slowing down your thoughts so you can go to sleep.) However, when we turn our attention to something that we can control, our ability to forget increases. I believe the same lesson applies to most chronic problems. As we become increasingly focused on the problem, we lose control. As we turn our attention to a higher goal, we gain control.

There is a story, often told, that has a similar message. It is the story of a widow who is overwhelmed by the sudden loss of her husband. Grief stricken, she tries every method she can think of to lessen her emotional pain. Finally a friend tells her of a potion maker who may help her with her suffering. She travels to the potion maker who expresses her regret that she has no potion to relieve intense sorrow. However, she does believe that the widow might find some relief if she were to find the happiest family in the nearby town and see if they have such a substance. Anxiously, the widow rushes to the largest house on the biggest hill in the town eagerly seeking the secret potion which will reduce her pain. There, the distinguished lady of the house listens carefully to the widow's story only to answer with a story of greater sadness herself. The widow listens but then goes to the next house continuing her quest. But here too she hears only of other's sorrows. Soon she forgets much of her own grieving as she comforts others—the potion she had been looking for.

Character can act as a potion. Concentration on character turns us to a higher order of thought and by doing so reduces our focus on problems that can eat away our lives. A "world view" that includes a personal list of our positive qualities that make up our character can be an extraordinary potion. Imagine facing the challenges we face in life with a strong belief in our own optimism, honesty, honor and integrity—qualities we may have but may not have acknowledged. If we don't presently believe these qualities are part of our make-up, we can become determined to make them so. Such a viewpoint puts a new perspective on the problem. No, it doesn't solve every problem. It may not make the problem go away, but what a starting point. Reminding ourselves of our internal character and what we stand for puts problems in a new light.

A word of caution. Maintaining a clear and solid picture of "who you are" and "what you stand for" is not always easy. It is important to throw certain qualifiers into the equation. None of us is perfect. We are all human with human frailties. We don't have enough information to solve many problems. "Committing ourself to take care of ourselves" should first of all include kindness to ourselves. Kindness, in turn, includes tolerance and forgiveness—two qualities critical to personal well-being.

Former President Harry Truman often publicly spoke as if he never looked back. In private, his biographer wrote, he had his moments of doubts. He simply never considered it helpful to dwell on decisions made. We all have our moments of doubt, our periods of insecurity. It would be an unusual man or woman who could look back on his or her life and feel that every decision was the right one. It is valuable to give ourselves the benefit of the doubt in most situations and consider that we did the best we could at the time with the knowledge and circumstances at hand. We are not perfect, but we can seek improvement.

You are about to finish reading a book on the topic of character and goodness. Hopefully you have been conscientious about doing the exercises. If you have, you have examined your identity and character from many directions. You began by describing yourself to a friend, thought about what people you admired and why. You may have promised yourself that you were going to learn more about those critical people so that you could follow their good examples even more often. Hopefully your sensitivity to the many positive qualities that can contribute to what we consider character and goodness has been increased and you have acknowledged that many fine qualities are in fact a part of your makeup. Perhaps you have also chosen to work on a few that need some attention—optimism, listening, and forgiving, for example. And maybe you have taken the affirmation written at the end of each chapter to heart and have even placed it in a highly visible setting.

If you have taken any of these actions you have joined in a time honored tradition of examining the best attributes of the human being, those characteristics of which we can feel most proud. I believe that wonderful qualities are spread across our families, our friends, our communities, and our nation. But they are too often like seeds that have gone unattended. They need to be watered and provided care. And when that happens, each seed gives pleasure to its immediate surroundings, bringing beauty to the countryside and to the entire land.

I'm doing my best to care of myself and I hope in some small way I have helped you to do the same.

I commit myself to take care of myself for the sake of myself, my family, my friends, my community and my country.

Suggested Reading Material

Bechtel, J. & Coughlin, R. *Building The Beloved Community*, Temple University Press, Philadelphia, 1991.

Covey, S. *The 7 Habits Of Highly Effective People*, Simon & Schuster, New York, NY, 1989.

Fischer, L. *The Life Of Mahatma Gandhi*, Harper & Row Publishers, New York, NY, 1950.

Frankl, V.E. *Man's Search For Meaning*, Simon & Schuster, New York, NY, 1984.

Gardner, H. *Leading Minds*, Basic Books, New York, NY, 1995.

Goleman, D. *Emotional Intelligence*, Bantam Book, New York, NY, 1995.

Goodwin, D.K. *No Ordinary Times*, Simon & Schuster, New York, NY, 1995.

Greer, C. & Kohl, H. (Eds.) *A Call To Character*, Harpercollins Publisher, New York, NY, 1995.

Kennedy, J.F. *Profiles In Courage*, Harper & Row, New York, NY, 1956.

Keller, H. *The Story Of My Life*, Bantam Books, New York, NY, 1988.

King, M.L., Jr. *Stride Toward Freedom*, HarperSanFrancisco, San Francisco, Cal., 1958.

Lash, J.P. *Helen And Teacher*, Addison-Wesley Publishing Co., Reading, Mass., 1980.

Maltz, M. *Psychocybernetics*, Prentice-Hall, New York, NY, 1960.

Mandela, N. *Long Walk To Freedom*, Little Brown & Co., Boston, Mass., 1994.

McCullough, D. *Truman*, Simon & Schuster, New York, NY, 1992.

Myers, D.G, *The Pursuit Of Happiness*, Avon Books, New York, NY, 1992.

Newman, M. & Berkowitz, B. *How To Be Your Own Best Friend*, Ballantine Books, New York, NY, 1971.

Ornish, D. *Love And Survival*, Hapercollins Press, New York, NY, 1997.

Pipher, M. *Reviving Ophelia*, Ballantine Books, New York, NY, 1995.

Pipher, M. *The Shelter Of Each Other*, Ballantine Books, New York, NY, 1996.

Real, T. *I Don't Want To Talk About It*, Scribner, New York, NY, 1997.

Robbins, A. *Awaken The Giant Within*, Summit Books, New York, NY, 1991.

Seligman, M.E *Learned Optimism*, Alfred A. Knopf. New York, NY, 1991.

Seligman, M.E. *What You Can Change & What You Can't*, Alfred A. Knopf. New York, NY, 1994.

Shorter, E. *From Paralysis To Fatigue*. The Free Press, New York, NY, 1992.

Williamson, M. *The Healing Of America* Simon & Schuster, New York, NY, 1997.

Wilson, E.O. *Naturalist,* Shearwater Books, Washington, D.C., 1994.

Wilson, R.A. (Ed.) *Character Above All,* Simon & Schuster, New York, NY, 1995.

Acknowledgement

I am forever grateful to my wife, Gail Scarbrough, for her unending support, editing and love.

About the author

ROBERT Pawlicki, Ph.D., a psychologist, lectures extensively and conducts workshops on practical means to find inner strength in meeting life's challenges. Formerly he was Director of the Behavioral Medicine Center at the Drake Center (a rehabilitation and long-term care hospital) in Cincinnati, Ohio and Pofessor at the University of Cincinnati College of Medicine. He is author of approximately 50 research and scholarly articles and the play *Mississippi Summer.* For more information see http://home.fuse.net/robertpawlicki/.

Endnotes

[1].Goodwin, D.K. *No Ordinary Time,* Simon & Schuster, New York, NY, 1995. page 565.

[2].McCullough, D. *Truman,* Simon & Schuster, New York, NY, 1992. page 55.

[3].Kennedy, J.F. *Profiles in Courage,* Harper & Row, New York, NY, 1956. page 249.

[4].McCullough, D. *Truman,* Simon & Schuster, New York, NY, 1992. page 54.

[5].Ibid., page 55.

[6].*A Testament Of Hope,* James M. Washington (Ed.), HarperSanFrancisco, San Francisco, CA, 1986.

[7].Ibid., page 77.

[8].This is a paraphrase of Gordon Alport's writing in the preface of Viktor Frankl's *Man's Search For Meaning,* Simon & Schuster, New York, NY, 1984.

[9].Keller, H. *The Story of My Life,* Bantam Books, New York, NY, 1988.

[10].From the film *Gandhi.*

[11.]Video tape: *America: Episode 6, "Fireball in the Night" with Allister Cook*, Produced by the BBC.

[12.]On June 12, 1962, Reverend McCrackin was defrocked and was restored to the pulpit of the Presbyterian church on Sept. 6, 1987.

[13.]*Readers Digest*, Oct. 97, page 124.

[14.]*The Cincinnati Post*, Dec. 6,1997.

[15.]Seligman, M.E. *What You Can Control And Things You Cannot*, Alfred A. Knopf, New York, NY, 1994.

[16.]Real, T. *I Don't Want to Talk About It*, Scribner, New York, NY, 1997. page 146.

[17.]Ibid.

[18.]Borysenko, J. & Borysenko, M. *The Power of the Mind to Heal*, Hay House Inc., Carson, CA, 1994. page 19.

[19.]Celente, G. *Trends 2000*, New York, NY, 1997. page 219.

[20.]Friedan, B. *Beyond Gender*, The Woodrow Wilson Center Press, Washington D.C., 1997.

[21.]Celente, G. *Trends 2000*, Warner Books, New York, NY, 1997. page 219.

[22.]*The Cincinnati Post*, December 30, 1997, page 3B.

[23.]Celente, G. *Trends 2000*, Warner Books, New York, NY, 1997. page 227.

[24.]Ornish, D. *Love And Survival*, HarperCollins, New York, NY, 1997.

[25.]Celente, G. *Trends 2000*, Warner Books, New York, NY, 1997. page 212.

[26.] Ibid., pages 212-213.

[27.]Pipher, M. *Reviving Ophelia*, Ballantine Books, New York, NY, 1995.

[28.]Ornish, D. *Love and Survival*, HarperCollins, New York, NY, 1997.

[29.]Borysenko J. & Borysenko, M. *The Power of the Mind to Heal*, Hay House, Carson CA., 1994. page 4.

[30.]Ibid., page 18.

[31.]Cited in Ornish, D. *Love And Survival*, HarpersCollins,

New York, NY, 1997. page 50.

[32.]Pipher, M. *Reviving Ophelia*, Ballantine Books, New York, NY, 1995. page 83.

[33.]Anthony Robbins' marvelous book *Awaken the Giant Within* has been an important book in my life and one I frequently recommend to friends and patients. His explanation of beliefs provided the basis in my own thoughts as I built the compilation of stories and exercises in this chapter.

[34.]Robbins, A. *Awaken the Giant Within*, Summit Books, New York, NY, 1991.

[35.]Covey, S. *The 7 Habits of Highly Effective People*, Simon & Schuster, New York, NY, 1989.

[36.]Ibid.

[37.]Fischer, L. *The Life of Mahatma Gandhi*, Harper & Row, New York, NY, 1950. pages 273-4

[38.]Ashe, A. *Days of Grace*, Ballantine Books, New York, NY, 1994.

[39.]Melzack, R. *The Puzzle of Pain*, Basic Books, New York, NY, 1973. page 22.

[40.]Morris, D. *The Culture of Pain*, University of California Press, Berkeley, CA., 1991.

[41.]Ibid.

[42.]Goodwin, D.K. Franklin D. Roosevelt: 1933-1945, In *Character Above All*, Robert A. Wilson, (Ed.) Simon & Schuster, New York, NY, 1995.

[43.]Goodwin, D.K. *No Ordinary Times*, Simon & Schuster, New York, NY, 1995. page 532.

[44.] *Time* Magazine, August 26, 1996.

[45.]Ibid.

[46.]Sheppard, W. & Willoughby *Child Behavior*, Rand McNally College Publishing Co., Chicago, 1975.

[47.]Pipher, M. *Reviving Ophelia*, Ballantine Books, New York, NY, 1995.

[48.]Ibid.

[49.]De Becker, G. *The Gift of Fear*, Little Brown, New York,

NY, 1997.

[50.]Cited in Pipher, M. *Reviving Ophelia*, Ballantine Books, New York, NY, 1995.

[51.]Ibid.

[52.]Newman, M. & Berkowitz, B. *How To Be Your Own Best Friend*, Ballantine Books, New York, NY, 1971. page 89.

[53.]Although self-confident people compliment themselves more, they may not necessarily say it out loud.

[54.]Kennedy, J.F. *Profiles in Courage*, Harper & Row, New York, NY, 1956. page 37.

[55.]Wilson, E.O. *Naturalist*, Shearwater Books, Washington, D.C. 1994. page 122.

[56.]Myers, D.J. *The Pursuit of Happiness*, Avon Books, New York, NY, 1992. page 177.

[57.]Seligman, M.E. *Learned Optimism*, Alfred A. Knopf, New York, NY, 1991.

[58.]Ibid. page 15.

[59.]Ibid. page 173.

[60.] *The Lincoln Library of Essential Information*, The Frontier Press Co., Buffalo, NY, 1953. page 534.

[61.]Ibid. page 551.

[62.]Fulghum, R. *Uh Oh*, Villard Books, New York, NY, 1991.

[63.]Frankl, V. *Man's Search For Meaning*, Simon & Schuster, New York, NY, 1984.

[64.] Ibid.

[65.]Morris, D. *The Culture of Pain*, University of California Press, Berkeley, CA., 1991. page 170.

[66.]Buscaglia, L. *Living, Loving and Learning*, Ballantine Books, New York, NY, 1982.

[67.]*Psychology Today*, July/August, 1994, Vol. 27(4), 34.

[68.]Riley, P. *The Winner Within*, G.P.Putnum & Son, New York, NY, 1993. page 161.

[69.]Kabat-Zenn, J. *Full Catastrophe Living*, Dell Publishing, New York, NY, 1990.

[70.]Blanchard, K. & Johnson, S. *The One Minute Manager*,

William Morrow & Co., New York, NY, 1982.

[71.]Riley, P. *The Winner Within*, G.P.Putnum & Son, New York, NY, 1993. page 161.

[72.]*Psychology Today*, July/August, 1994, Vol. 27(4), 34.

[73.]Dr. Gonzoles—I don't believe I ever knew his first name.

[74.]I have been making 20 to 40 speeches annually for the past ten years.